Reviews for *On Warne*

'Gideon Haigh's slim, elegant book *On Warne* has its own kind of confidence . . . Haigh is an excellent essayist.' Ed Smith, *New Statesman*

'On Warne comes from the pen of the most gifted cricket essayist of his generation, and this short book forms as shrewd and entertaining a portrait as the era's outstanding cricketer deserves, with moments of brilliant description . . . amusing and perceptive.' Richard Williams, *Guardian*

'Bloody brilliant . . . The second chapter in particular . . . is as good as anything I have read on the game . . . Haigh cuts out the extraneous information and concentrates on the essence.' Andy Bull, *Guardian*

'The best cricketer of his generation deconstructed by the best cricket writer of his . . . This is a masterful book: affectionate yet detached, ceaselessly insightful yet formidably well written . . . Perhaps it is a cliché to refer to a biography as definitive; in this case it would be remiss not to do so.' Rob Smyth, *The Cricketer*

'Haigh's book is small but perfectly pitched. He has chosen one of the most magnetic sportsmen of the last 20 years, and he sees Shane Warne from every angle.' *Daily Telegraph*

'It's Haigh's analysis of Warne himself that inevitably, and rightly, steals the show . . . My favourite Haigh book to date, and frankly there have been a few.' *All Out Cricket*

'Cricket has taken a back seat this summer, but there were two outstanding books about the game. *On Warne* by Gideon Haigh has a philosophical, essayist title for a tract by Australia's finest cricket writer on the greatest and most flamboyant spin bowler in history.' *The Times*

'An affectionate yet judicious study that will probably never be surpassed.' David Hopps, *Cricinfo*

'Cricket has always attracted good writers, and the Australian journalist Gideon Haigh is undoubtedly among the finest at work today . . . *On Warne* is not a conventional biography but rather a characteristically sharp and elegant analysis of the Warne phenomenon.' *Times Literary Supplement*

'A conventional biography would somehow obscure Warne's story. A cricket writer as peerless as Haigh knows this. Haigh's is an exquisite treatment . . . his eye for relevant detail is astonishing . . . You get the feeling that Haigh understands Warne's mastery better than Warne himself, and he never fails to capture it crisply . . . Warne's wizardry is rich enough to unleash Haigh's, and Haigh's wizardry brings Warne's to life anew.' Waleed Aly, *The Monthly*

'Haigh's utterly addictive book traces how and why Warne became different . . . A marvellous analysis of the Warne mystique and the prodigious talent feeding it. This is cricket writing as art, turning the creative leaps familiar in fiction or literary non-fiction to the task of anatomising the ungraspable nature of genius. *On Warne* is a sublime treat.' Brian Matthews, *Australian Book Review*

'Haigh's brilliant turn of phrase is mesmerising. He manages to be neither assassin nor cheerleader in his examination of the cricketing great. Rather than a bland biography, this is a study of what makes Warne a sometimes tragic, often amusing, usually polarising and always intriguing figure.' Scott Moore, *The Advertiser* (Adelaide)

'An intimate study of one of the greatest cricketers of the modern era . . . Haigh writes with perception and humour . . . A book to be savoured now and into the future.' Peter Crossing, *Canberra Times*

'The Bradman of cricket writing spins us a yarn with deftness, skill and intrigue.' Taylor Auerbach, *Sunday Telegraph*

About the author

Gideon Haigh is one of the world's best-known cricket writers. He has been a journalist for almost thirty years, writing about sport and business, and has contributed to more than 100 newspapers and magazines. *On Warne* is his twenty-sixth book. His website is www.gideonhaigh.com.

GIDEON HAIGH
ON
WARNE

**SIMON &
SCHUSTER**

London · New York · Sydney · Toronto · New Delhi

A CBS COMPANY

First published in Great Britain by Simon & Schuster UK Ltd, 2012
This paperback edition published by Simon & Schuster UK Ltd, 2013

A CBS COMPANY

1 3 5 7 9 10 8 6 4 2

Simon & Schuster UK Ltd
1st Floor
222 Gray's Inn Road
London
WC1X 8HB

www.simonandschuster.co.uk

Simon & Schuster Australia, Sydney
Simon & Schuster India, New Delhi

A CIP catalogue for this book is available
from the British Library.

ISBN: 978-1-47110-111-3
Ebook ISBN: 978-47110-112-0

Designed by John Canty
Printed and bound by CPI Group (UK) Ltd, Croydon, CR0 4YY

CONTENTS

ONE

THE MAKING OF
WARNE

WARNIE: he was always Warnie. You can thank television for that – all those exhalations of 'Bowled, Warnie' from Ian Healy filtered through the pitch microphones. But it suited him. After all, you could hardly call him Warne. One syllable, origin Cornish. No, you needed that little Australian tick at the end, in the spirit of prezzy, telly and rellie, identifying him as ours, and also making him everyone's. Because everyone knew about whom you were talking, didn't they? Yes, other cricketers have been identifiable by nicknames, but 'The Don' was to ennoble Donald Bradman, 'AB' partly to reflect Allan Border's primacy. Warnie? It was familiar, playful, companionable. It was the sort of appellation you might attach to a cricket clubmate, a workmate, or even just a mate in general. I'm catching up with Warnie tonight. Warnie's coming over tomorrow. You'll never guess what Warnie's done now.

Warnie was likewise never other than himself. There might at first have been a desire to fit him into the continuum of Australian wrist spin: Hordern, Mailey, Grimmett, O'Reilly, Benaud, etc. But he was never the new Benaud, and certainly never the next Bob Holland or the coming Jim Higgs. When he made his Test debut, he actually looked like that friend of a friend who turns up to help your club out on Saturday, who used to play but hasn't for ages, who didn't have anything on and thought it might be fun to have a bit of a run-around, albeit he'd had a few the night before and maybe you could put him somewhere quiet. Warne completed the parallel by turning up to his first public appearance as an Australian player badly hung-over, reporting afterwards: 'I headed straight for the safety of the toilet but didn't make it in time.'

No, there was not really a lineage for him to join that day – probably the opposite. When they took the field together, Allan Border actually invoked a less happy memory. 'Don't do a Johnny Watkins on us,' he urged – a reference to the luckless leg-break bowler who had panicked at his only Test outing twenty years before. It was not, perhaps, the most sensitive of allusions, but there was a certain rough-house humour to it, as well as some worldly wisdom. What you're about to do is difficult. What you're about to do will test your resilience, and now and again you may cop a hiding. But don't drop your bundle, because nobody else will pick it up.

And while it was one of those days a hiding came his way, Warnie did as he was bidden, and within eighteen months had the cricket world at his feet, having bowled what was instantly dubbed 'the Ball of the Century'. He was twenty-three – a young twenty-three, too, with little education, little self-awareness, still leading a sheltered life at home. The cultural historian Leo Braudy has observed that those who succeed in youth sometimes become symbolic before they become real – that one is 'created by others before one can create oneself'. Yet the 'Warnie' persona appeared to rest lightly on him: a bit flash, a bit lairy, everyone's mischievous pal, everyone's incorrigible kid brother. So it was that even as he wrote the book on leg spin, he also wrote the book on fame.

In our age, only two other cricketers have enjoyed comparable renown, dealing with it rather differently. Sachin Tendulkar veered one way, preserving his excellence by sequestering himself from a clamouring public; Ian Botham veered the other, allowing his legendary self-belief to become self-parodic. Warnie swaggered down the middle of the road, living large but always bowling big, revelling in the attention while never losing the love of his craft, seeming to treat the tabloid exposés as lightheartedly as sixes hit off his bowling. Just an occupational hazard. He'd put things right soon enough.

In doing so, he became Australia's best-known sportsman; perhaps even the most recognised Australian. Yet for all that visibility, large parts remained out of view – perhaps even to himself. 'I am pretty simple, I think, don't you?' he proposed when interviewed by Jana Wendt in 2006, only to respond when she questioned him about his aberrations of behaviour: 'A lot of people don't understand. I don't understand.' She left, like many an interviewer before and since, concluding that it was 'uncommonly easy to like him and a little harder to explain why'. I know exactly what Wendt means.

I first met Shane Warne when I interviewed him for *Inside Sport* magazine in June 1994, at the end of a year in which he had become not only cricket's outstanding slow bowler, but its biggest headline producer. He had contributed the Ball of the Century to cricket folklore; he had been damned for a display of petulance after taking the wicket of Andrew Hudson in Johannesburg; he was about to undertake the tour on which he would make the acquaintance of 'John the bookie'. A publicity soundtrack had begun to which his deeds and misdeeds would form a drumbeat of praise and blame. Awaiting him in a bar in the Melbourne suburb of Brighton, I was not quite sure what to expect, and I confess after all these years I am still bemused by my first impression, which was of his excellent manners.

Warne arrived talking on one of those cumbrous old mobile phones, which he snapped off with a 'Gotta go, mate' as soon as our eyes met, so that he could offer a big, thick-fingered hand. I braced myself for the bear-like grasp common among Australian sporting males, but did not receive it. The greeting was easy, open, genial. He apologised for being five minutes late – he had been filming a segment for *Burke's Backyard*. He asked if I'd had trouble finding the place – some people did. Some years later when I read

Primary Colors, the description of Governor Jack Stanton's warm and intimate greeting 'with that famous misty look' struck me as an almost perfect description of meeting Warne. And Stanton is, of course, modelled on Bill Clinton, a man of similar charm, presence and susceptibilities to Warne.

'Beer?' Warne suggested, moving towards the bar, although when I explained I didn't drink he bought softies instead. 'Mind if I have a cigarette?' he asked as we adjourned to a nearby table, and I said I'd be only too pleased as I also smoked; later on, when I ran out, he gave me his spare packet. 'I've got heaps,' he explained – golden days, indeed, when Benson & Hedges was still Australian cricket's sponsor, and free cigarettes abounded.

The interview unfolded much as five subsequent ones at intervals over Warne's career. There was barely any need to get him started; if anything, you needed to slow him down a mite, so swiftly did his answers tend to gallop away from your original inquiry. Warne wasn't to be fenced in by a question. He proceeded in a direction generally answerwards, and it was your job to keep up. I enjoyed it. In fact, I enjoyed every aspect of talking to Warne, not least his inexhaustible enthusiasm for cricket. I always listened with an ear cocked for any hint that he might be jaded, or bored, or fed up, or going through the motions, but never heard anything of the kind.

I should perhaps have been more surprised about this enjoyment than I was, in that we had little in common beyond the cricket and maybe the smoking too. But really: he was big, beamish, talkative, fun; I was skinny, geeky, bookish and earnest. A few years later, I'd write a book about a spin bowler from the same suburb, Jack Iverson, who was doubting, diffident, self-torturing, and eventually self-destructive; I would have found it difficult to explain that life, and my interest in it, to Warne. But there he was: thoroughly engaging, not to say troublingly so, because it's best in journalism not to like your subjects too much, lest you forget the roles of the respective parties. There's a story about the left-wing journalist Paul Foot returning to the office of *Private Eye* from an interview with the right-wing politician and polemicist Enoch Powell in the early 1970s, putting his head down on the desk and groaning: 'Oh, God . . . I liked him! I liked him!' I'm bound to say that it was harder to set this aside with Warne than almost anyone I have interviewed.

We spoke on that first occasion for around two hours, and it was I who ended the conversation, vaguely aware he had somewhere to be. Two things stick in my mind. As we shook hands by the exit, Warne asked abruptly: 'Was I what you expected?' The tone was not egotistical or aggrandising; it was the inquiry of someone just getting used to the idea that the impression he made on people was something that mattered, but over which he had limited control. I can't remember my reply, but I recall his next comment: 'The trouble is, people I've never met think they know all about me.' Again, it wasn't a bitter or a self-pitying remark; it was someone thinking aloud as they accustomed themselves to an idea. From that point forward, I always wondered about the long-term impact of never meeting anyone who did not know already who one was, who did not come with preconceptions, expectations, demands, annoyances. Warne would over the years admit to a certain vanity – indeed, the confession was integral to his defence against charges he had taken a banned substance. Was this partly an outcome, I speculated, of a reputation and recognisability that preceded Warne everywhere, a sense of having something to live up to, a desire not to disappoint?

The other recollection is of standing at the stop soon afterwards awaiting my tram when at the traffic lights pulled up a RAV4 – the car Warne had won a few months earlier for being International Cricketer of the Year. 'Need a lift anywhere, Gideon?' said Warne, leaning out his window. I thought quickly. Was this ethical? Would I be accepting a favour that obligated me to my interviewee, that might compromise my objectivity? I decided I had better not, and declined the offer. 'You sure?' he asked. 'Okay, no worries.' His car pulled away and vanished into the night. An hour later I was still standing there – such is public transport in Melbourne – although the time passed quite quickly. I spent it wondering what I had struck.

We are all of us *still* wondering – thus this book. I court his disapproval in undertaking it, because Warne is on record as saying that it should be illegal to write about someone without their permission – and, surprisingly perhaps, I have some sympathy with this point of view. 'Isn't this a simple matter?' asked Doris Lessing, when submitted to the scrutiny of an unwelcome biographer. 'There are people who like to be biographied, but the ones who refuse, may we not be excused? After all, we will be dead soon enough.' A writer, moreover, is at least guaranteed some control of their works by copyright; the athlete enjoys no such protection.

This book is not, however, a life story, which can seemingly contain few remaining surprises given the cumulative journalistic efforts to lay them bare, and has in any event been laid out at book length on at least fifteen occasions, most recently, sneeringly and priggishly by Paul Barry. This is an examination of Warne's craft, an analysis of his career, and a survey of his phenomenon, while I'm still able to remember what it was like to live through all of them. Perhaps it is inevitable that Warne the cricketer will eventually be effaced in collective memory by Warne the image, but in the meantime some worthwhile purpose seems served by trying to reclaim him as a sportsman. We may not see his like again. We very nearly did not see him.

Shane Warne, commences nearly every attempt to retell his story, is a boy from the burbs. The expression is rather less than meaningful, given that around 90 per cent of residents of Australia's capital cities live more than five kilometres from their respective central business districts. But the point usually being made is that Warne is like everyone else – a contention with positive and pejorative connotations. Australia is a country, it has been said, whose people crave the approval of their garbage collector. Nobody wishes to be seen as too high and mighty; there is a pride taken in treating all alike.

Warne values his membership of this egalitariat, nurtures his common touch, boasts of his inattention and irreverence at school, likes people to know he has 'never read a complete book' in his life and that he prefers to curl up with a good phone; in suburbia's fictionalised arcadias, from *Neighbours* to *Kath & Kim,* he has looked very much at home. All of which plays to the stereotype of the suburbs as bastions of a white, materialist, anti-intellectual middle class. Australian thinkers, noted the economist Hugh Stretton, have tended to decry and essentialise their suburbs with 'especial anger or gloom'; by identifying so cheerfully with them, Warne was in some eyes almost born to be suspect.

The typicality of his youth, it must be said, does seem to run rather more than skin-deep. Warne was born at the Angliss Hospital in sylvan Ferntree Gully on 13 September 1969, but by the time he was school age his family had wended their way to Melbourne's bayside suburbs, first Hampton, then Black Rock – a conventional migration, given the identification of access to sea and surf with the Australian leisure class. The constant presence in Warne's life was probably his German-born mother Brigitte, three years old when her family joined the waves of postwar European migration to Australia. She is by all accounts a feisty, energetic, outgoing woman, dedicated to her sons, Shane and his younger brother Jason.

In the late 1960s and early 1970s, writers such as the journalist Craig McGregor and the sociologist Ronald Conway were hypothesising that Australia should be considered not a patriarchy but a 'matriduxy', women having essentially usurped the Australian male in the domestic sphere by taking control of household finances, social organisation and child rearing. 'All this fits in with everyday evidence about Australian families,' argued McGregor. 'The father appears to be the centre of authority, but when one of the children wants to do something the reply is often "Go and ask your mother" or "If it's all right with Mum, it's all right with me".' Imagining such an arrangement in the Warne household doesn't require a great stretch.

The influence of Shane's softly spoken father Keith, however, is not to be underestimated. He was a financial services consultant, successful enough to indulge a love of prestige marques. Keith was not a cricketer; rather, he took it up aged forty when Shane and Jason showed aptitude, in order to play alongside them at East Sandringham Boys Cricket Club in the City of Moorabbin Cricket Association; the father took after the sons rather than the sons the father. It was a secure but liberal household, of opportunity, fun and forgiveness.

A lot has been postulated about the role of Warne's upbringing in the man he became. In setting up a straw Warne in his *Spun Out,* for example, Paul Barry speculates that 'something in those early years' must gnaw at him, although Barry doesn't really know what it is, and scarcely cares: he simply has 540 pages to fill, and it may seem a more worthwhile expenditure of his energies if he sets up lame oppositions like 'walking paradox' and 'a genius locked in the body of a fool'. On the contrary, Warne seems to have had a very happy childhood in a contented and harmonious household, and to have retained his bourgeois preferences as a member of the beau monde: plain tastes, good manners, treating people at face value and elders with respect. In time, he put love, comfort and security to the use we would actually always intend for them: as a base for achieving something noteworthy. It's almost unusual for being so simple.

So happy was his childhood that Warne would probably have been content for it to continue indefinitely: certainly his life took a trajectory that nurtured what he once described as the 'big kid inside me who likes to have fun'. No epicure, he retained a childlike diet, heavy on cheese, bread, pizza and sweet drinks. He maintained a youthful enthusiasm for bright and shiny toys, inheriting his father's love of cars. He has always been happy propped in front of a television, and to this day the walls of his home are hung with more screens than artworks. He even maintained a teen-film fetish long into adulthood – thus his famous sledge of England's Ian Bell, likening him to the 'Sherminator', the buck-toothed ginger in *American Pie*. Plus, of course, he gravitated to sport, among whose many purposes, the social critic Christopher Lasch noted, is a kind of staving off or at least negotiation of change, recreating 'the remembered perfection of childhood' within 'artificial boundaries', satisfying both 'the need for free fantasy and the search for gratuitous difficulty'.

Sport also held forth its abiding Australian promise – of social mobility. Warne's upbringing has lent itself to ready-made contrast with Bradman's, who is perhaps to the bush as Warne is to the burbs. Bradman is usually held up as the embodiment of solitary drive and youthful perfectionism, Warne as the spoiled party boy almost too companionable for his own good. In fact, the views say as much about our received images of their origins as anything: the bush as a home to the authentic Australian spirit, the burbs its sterile, phoney, derivative replacement. For both achieved through sport their first glimmers of recognition from the wider world, eighteen-year-old Bradman when he was invited to Sydney by the St George Cricket Club, fifteen-year-old Warne when he was awarded a sporting scholarship to Mentone Grammar. They then turned these opportunities to separate and distinct ends, Bradman through single-minded dedication to cricket's most elemental act, that of hitting the ball, Warne through an uncanny mastery of cricket's most complicated and challenging art, that of spinning the ball.

Who can tell why Warne should have elected to pursue wrist spin? Instructed in the leg break at East Sandringham, he did not take to it at once: 'I've no idea why I stuck with it. I could never land the bloody thing then.' He was initially, he has said, simply curious, made so by watching senior practice at the club, and the way that some bowlers 'could make the ball spin either way without my being able to spot the difference'. But he preferred batting, and not without reason.

Slow bowling is the most speculative and venturesome of all cricket's activities. 'I cannot approve of his recommending a young player to give a twist to his balls,' counselled John Nyren 180 years ago in his canonical text, *The Young Cricketer's Tutor*. 'For in the first place, there are a hundred chances against his accomplishing the art, and ten hundred in favour of the practice spoiling his bowling altogether.' Of all slow bowling's variants, leg spin is the most enchanting, frustrating and confounding. 'Leg spinners pose problems much like love,' wrote Alan Ross in his poem 'Watching Benaud Bowl'. 'Requiring commitment/The taking of a chance.' And in the decade Shane Warne began to play, cricket was less about love than sex: the sex of speed. In the 1980s, every country's glass of fashion was the unassailable West Indies, with their devastating fast-bowling array – prowling, predatory, subtly erotic.

It was, all the same, safe sex. For all its red-blooded virility, fast bowling reflected an attritional approach, which Australia was minded to mimic. When the West Indies picked four pace bowlers, we picked four too: it was the *professional* thing to do, the percentage strategy; it kept things tight and slowed the game, so if we didn't win we at least didn't lose as quickly. Although Australia twice took dead Tests off the West Indies in Sydney with slow bowling on helpful pitches, these were consolation victories; it barely occurred to us that Tests could be won by similar artifice on a regular basis.

The barren scene for leg spin was relieved only by Abdul Qadir, Pakistan's gremlin of the googly, with varieties beyond number, if just one appeal, beseeching and protracted. But Qadir took only 68 wickets at a costly 48 runs each away from home, where he was exhibited rather like a zookeeper's prize – the last example in captivity of *Homo googlius*, formerly widespread, now confined to a single habitat. Through the 1980s, spin was described dolefully. 'What hope for spin?' asked Pat Murphy in *The Spinner's Turn*. 'Where have all the spinners gone?' wondered Fred Trueman and Trevor Bailey in *The Spinners' Web*. *Spinning in a Fast World* was the defeatist title of John Emburey's guidebook.

In Australia, the pang of absence was most acute. On our flat, hard, sun-baked pitches, off breaks have ever been a mug's game; slow bowling has been about leg breaks and googlies, spun harder, usually bowled slower, generally both a little more penetrative and also expensive. Yet the great chain of practitioners, anchored by

Ranji Hordern, progenitor of the googly in Australia at the dawn of the twentieth century, had broken down. Arthur Mailey and Clarrie Grimmett were names in books. Bill O'Reilly had staked out a miserabilist corner of the *Sydney Morning Herald* in which a pet peeve was the decadence and dreariness of a game without wrist spin. If you've a good cricket memory now, you can recite some of the decade's could-be-anythings, anointed too soon, gone before their time: Malcolm Dolman, Chris Broadby, Adrian Tucker, Stuart Saunders, Stephen Milosz, to name but a few.

Yet here is the wonder of it. The most exorbitantly talented leg-break bowler in history largely eluded not just cricket's notice but his own. Warne wanted, first and foremost, to be a foot-baller – and not just any footballer, but a blond-haired star like St Kilda's Trevor Barker and Hawthorn's Dermott Brereton. In fact, he lacked the talent, the physique and the work ethic to go further than the reserves at St Kilda, being unceremoniously cut from its list at the end of the 1988 season. In the meantime, he was neither O'Reilly, wheeling away for hour upon hour with a mallee root when there was no ball to hand, nor po-faced Mailey, who never saw an orange he did not want to spin, nor wizened Grimmett, who made a willing slave of his fox terrier during solitary practice sessions. Slow bowling was what Warne was left with when his original ambitions peeled away.

Perhaps it was a help rather than a hindrance: he could ignore the dire forebodings about spin's future as he grew up, forget the occasional sloggings that mark every young spinner's career, pursue his ends by exquisite indirection, developing a distance from his craft, a natural perspective, a philosophical streak. He could continue treating it almost as a parlour game: look how far he could spin the ball!

Warne has turned 'cricket found me' into a cliché. 'I have skill as a cricketer, and, fortunately, cricket found me,' his high-definition 3D simulacrum repeats every fifteen minutes at the National Sports Museum at the Melbourne Cricket Ground. And there is no mistaking that, to the man himself, the idea has been deeply empowering. Great sport stories often ooze the loneliness of excellence, the pain of perfectionism. 'Many athletes seem truly to love to play their sport,' said John McEnroe in his autobiography. 'I don't think I ever felt that way about tennis.' Andre Agassi owned to hating tennis 'with a dark and secret passion'. Even the averagely gifted recognise the compulsive aspect in their psychologies. 'You spend a good piece of your life gripping a baseball,' remarked Jim Bouton in his classic journeyman's journal *Ball Four*. 'And it turns out it was the other way round all the time.' Warne, by contrast, keen but not desperate, enthused but investing little of himself, walked backwards into his future. Had he but known it, he was developing an ideal leg spinner's constitution.

Warne was also arriving at the physicality to go with it. He grew evenly to 180 centimetres, without suffering the growth spurt that unsettles many young slow bowlers by changing their natural trajectories. He came by a husky upper body, thanks partly to a childhood accident that simultaneously broke both his legs and for nearly a year confined him to a cart in which he had to push himself around. If not speedy, his legs themselves were strong, suited to conveying him from A to B all the live long day. And for all the jests and jollies about Warne's body during his cricket career, he was in general, in the original sense of the word, perfectly 'fit' – fitted to his task, suited to his skills.

Warne was in some respects like that old joke about the Australian asked if he can play the violin. 'I don't know,' the Aussie answers. 'I've never tried.' As Warne's career unfolded, so did the wonder grow of its serendipity, bordering on preordination. Cricket found him, he would say, as though it had been out there looking all along.

That he was a good junior cricketer and not a precocious one who shattered records left and right may also have grounded him more firmly in the game, rather than wedding him to a particular faculty. Because Warne from the first exhibited an affinity with all of cricket. He bowled leg breaks, but he also bowled medium-pace, hit hard, caught well, and captained successfully, at Mentone Grammar. He watched too. He was exposed to cricket's celebrity pull: the first one-day game he attended was one of Kerry Packer's attractions at VFL Park. He absorbed cricket's element of speculation: the first Test he saw was the 1982 Boxing Day match, on the final morning of which Australian hopes were carried by last pair Allan Border and Jeff Thomson, who had added 37 and needed 37 more for victory. Here was the quintessential anything-could-happen Test day. One ball could have ended it. Yet the hopeful thousands who trekked to Jolimont were rewarded with an hour of perfect agony ending three runs short of ecstasy – twelve years later, those who flocked to the ground despite the foregone conclusion of another one-sided Ashes Test were gifted by Warne with a hat-trick.

Warne was imbued with the game, then, rather than simply

infatuated with one dimension of it – his own, rather anachronistic facility for turning the ball from leg to off. He did not have to identify with Jim Higgs or Bob Holland or Peter Sleep or Trevor Hohns, or any of the other triers who preserved the guttering flame of leg spin in Australia through the 1980s; he could enjoy the game for its possibilities, drift along on its dreams, explain that he was playing 'because my mates did'. The happy-go-lucky impression he gives of himself in his various life stories suggests someone who would have been deterred by anything at which he had to try too hard, anything demanding total immersion. Even when his football career petered out, he does not seem to have committed himself to cricket: it was something he did, rather than who he was. He returned from a northern summer of club cricket in England's West Country so overweight that his father almost failed to recognise him at the airport. And he might very easily have slipped from sight altogether but for the tide in Australian cricket's affairs.

In a true and arguably unprecedented historic sense, cricket *did* find Warne. He was taken in by the game as he floated through it because of a unique set of circumstances; and that embrace was an outcome not of success but of compound failure, in sport in general, and cricket in particular.

Traditionally, Australia had relied for its sporting exemplars on the admixture of talent, sun, fresh air and open space. It came in for a rude awakening at the 1976 Montreal Olympics, where its athletes failed to win a gold medal for the first time in four decades, plunging the national sports establishment into introspection. A writer in *The Guardian* likened the country to a 'middle-aged athlete gone flabby', and as a consequence 'stricken by self-doubt and torn by bitter recriminations'. The toning up recommenced with the foreshadowing in January 1980 of an Australian Institute of Sport, which opened the following year to 153 'scholars' with the prime ministerial promise that the country was 'no longer going to let the rest of the world pass us by'.

Yet that was exactly what happened in Australian cricket in the ensuing nine years, a phase as barren as any in its history. The loss of three in four Ashes series, and four in five Frank Worrell Trophy series aroused interest in a cricket academy as part of the AIS, and dedicated to a similar kind of hothousing of talent. The country's new national coach, Bob Simpson, was in favour; so was an individual who thought himself a kind of national coach, cricket-loving prime minister Bob Hawke; so was the Commonwealth Bank, still state-owned and patriotically oriented. The Australian Cricket Board determined the inaugural intake of scholars at a training camp in September 1987, and managers Jack Potter and Peter Spence began running their residential programme from an AIS office on Adelaide's Henley Beach Road eight months later.

Crisis, as they say, begets opportunity. It's quite possible that a successful Australian team in the 1980s would have militated against the rise of Shane Warne, that there would not then have been a compulsion to beat the country's bushes for cricket talent, that with his vagrant spirit he would have slowly departed from the scene. Twenty when he made his first XI debut at the district club of St Kilda in December 1989, he would in the normal run of events have achieved little notice, taking as he did only nine expensive wickets in his eleven games that season. Instead, Warne benefited not only from the reform of the Australian game, but also from its still personal nature, for he was passed along an old-fashioned cricket chain: after watching Warne in the nets at St Kilda one night, Test selector Jim Higgs urged Potter and Spence to take him on as an extra 'scholar' – perhaps the first and only time the word has been used in the context of Warne. Despite his being a year or two older than the rest, they welcomed him in April 1990.

The rationale was simple: Warne gave it a rip. Leaving his hand, the ball emitted an audible *flit-flit-flit-flit*, then on descending to earth deviated as much as half a pitch's width. It did not always land where it was aimed; the unplayable was interspersed with the unreachable. But for all the learned nostrums about the need for precision and consistency that are usually stressed around young spinners, nothing excites other cricketers more in evaluating potential than a massive break, because nothing is more innate. A spinner can grow smarter, tighter, more various, more aggressive, but because the imparting of spin is as much an outcome of physicality as a matter of skill, seldom will they learn to impart more revs. If anything, the opposite is likelier – that revs will be sacrificed in pursuit of accuracy, or lost in the passage of years. While Warne's young technique was still embryonic – he had at first an old-fashioned rock-back action, approaching slowly, tossing it high – what could not be taught was always there.

In hindsight, he had unconsciously imbibed one of sport's

first principles. Jack Nicklaus's advice to every young golfer has been to learn to drive the ball a long way and only then to think about getting it in the hole; Rafa Nadal's coach counselled him early on simply to hit the ball hard and only then to concern himself with keeping it in; without needing to be told, Warne rejoiced in the tricks a rotating sphere could play. It did not have to be a cricket ball. He would whiz tennis balls down the corridor of his digs at the Alberton Hotel, and whirr billiard balls round its pool table – spinning leg breaks into the left corner pocket and wrong'uns into the right – then, when Potter taught him a fiendishly difficult variation called the flipper, making balls spin back as well. Few cricketers, then, could have blended more perfectly with the academy's mission, to mould Test cricketers out of inchoate, untamed talent. Rough, raw but rich in possibility, Warne was in a sense a coach's dream.

Warne was also, proverbially, a coach's nightmare. His time at the academy has been amply mythologised, partly by him. He is the rebel soul who bucked the system, the maverick genius à rebours. He certainly looked the part, with his casual indifference to training, sunny sense of entitlement, invariably bulging billfold supplemented from home, and hotted-up white Cortina with sun roof and mag wheels. On the day that his future teammates Justin Langer and Damien Martyn first met him, he was sitting alone devouring a family-sized pizza and supping on a can of VB. Unlike contemporaries such as Michael Slater, who pursued a place at the academy as though his life depended on it, Warne emanated a sense that his was an opportunity to take or leave. But perhaps because these were early days in the experiment, this did not work against him as it later might have. His puerile excesses tested the patience of his elders but never to breaking point, partly because everyone was feeling their way in this new regime, and partly because Potter and Spence had rather more to deal with behind the scenes than Warne's indiscretions.

Surprisingly in hindsight, Potter and Spence had at this stage few allies. Promised government monies did not eventuate. Older cricket salts thought the academy, with its emphasis on fitness and athleticism, too scientific and experimental; their idea of coaching was still practice nets and high catches. For their part, the AIS bureaucracy found cricket old-fashioned, and disapproved of the academy's connection with the Commonwealth Bank; what was the institute doing helping a wealthy sport like cricket anyway? Potter and Spence found themselves tugged this way then that, and finally quit, after which there was an attempt to introduce more traditional coaching discipline, against which Warne predictably chafed; the AIS then bungled the probation Warne was placed on, and he finally resolved the stand-off by returning to Melbourne. The official history of the AIS does not even mention cricket, disowning in a way its most famous product.

Because Warne became Warnie, much has been made of his follies at the academy, although what they betray as much as anything is the awkwardness of the cultural shift from old ways to new. The irony is that the casual Warne achieved his first recognition through the new system, which struggled to deal with him, then came to an accommodation with the old system, which did not regard his failure to fit in with all this newfangled jiggery-pokery all that severely. And far from being a headstrong individualist,

Warne was in many ways as anxious to fit in as anyone of his age. Because he liked to be liked, he took to bleaching his hair, self-conscious about the natural strawberry-blond tinge of his locks which had led to his being nicknamed variously 'Twistie' and 'Bloodnut'. Because he liked to be useful, he tried quite hard at being a part-time file clerk at the South Australian Cricket Association. And because he had much to offer, exceptions were made – including one very large one.

Events have imbued the meeting of Warne and Terry Jenner with a sort of Stanley-meets-Livingstone quality. But it was intriguing before it was momentous. This was the new regime deferring somewhat to the old. Jenner was as in touch with the ethos of athleticism as he was with the tenets of postmodern literary theory. He was an old cricketer, and down on his luck as well. After nine intermittent Test matches in the 1970s, he had quit too young and found himself adrift, with a deficient formal education, an employment history of more than forty different jobs, from railway clerk to towbar salesman, and a costly gambling habit. For bilking one caryard employer to fund it he had received a suspended sentence; for bilking a second he had been sent for a long prison stretch. In introducing the pair, Spence was perhaps as concerned as much about Jenner's rehabilitation as Warne's habilitation.

As they were coming to know one another, both were men on trial. Jenner remained on parole; Warne was on a final warning about his behaviour, following the misdemeanour of swearing at Potter's replacement, Barry Causby, on a sandhill run. Warne may have responded to Jenner better because the older man was hardly in a position to issue moral lessons. For all his immense knowledge of the fact and folklore of leg spin, 'TJ' was a diffident man with whom slights had always resonated. He never forgot Australian selector Neil Harvey saying that he himself could have handled Jenner one-handed. 'He probably could,' Jenner confided. 'But I wish he hadn't said it.' On even the highlights of his career Jenner was inclined to look back ambivalently. Of what he thought was the best ball he ever bowled, which beat Garry Sobers through the gate, Jenner mused: 'I couldn't believe it was me.'

We are accustomed to thinking of the coach–player relationship as being an analogue either of parenthood or of education, or even of the military. But at least at first, Jenner's rapport with Warne had no such quality; on the contrary. As Warne put it in his autobiography, in a rather infelicitous juxtaposition: 'I think I immediately recognized a kindred spirit. At that time he had recently left prison after serving eighteen months for embezzlement.' As much as Jenner had to teach Warne about leg spin, perhaps his most immediate lesson was in what not to do – with one's skill, with one's career, with one's life. The relationship came to be based not around Warne's reverence for Jenner, but around Jenner's sincere reverence for Warne – or, at least, for Warne's gift, because it was this that allowed him to place personal affection to one side and to stress the young man's responsibility to fulfil his potential. There can hardly have been a more significant private conversation in the annals of Australian cricket than the one between Warne and Jenner about eighteen months after their introduction.

Jenner's induction in Warne's ways followed a standard cycle. He was excited and fascinated by the potential; he was engaged and charmed by the personality; he looked askance at the application, while hardly being best placed to fault anyone on a failure to make the most of their talent. The pair built a warm bond. Jenner was worldly but reticent; as Warne put it, he 'suggested' rather than imposed. That enabled Warne to feel not only improved but also justified in his disillusionment with the academy: didn't they understand that he responded to the carrot rather than the stick? Coach and charge then saw results from their collaboration, when Warne was chosen for his first senior tour, to Zimbabwe with an Australia B team, and a maiden Test, at Sydney, thereby becoming the first academy alumnus to make the grade in international cricket.

The initiation, against India at the Sydney Cricket Ground, was a harsh one. Tenderfoot Warne was stamped on, by Ravi Shastri and Sachin Tendulkar, in the last 25 of his 45 overs giving up almost a run a ball. Worse, he looked like a 97-kilogram stumblebum roped in from the beach, 'lucky' yellow speedos visible through the white pants that did not match his cream shirt. But leg spin in a Test match in Australia was such a fresh and welcome sight that judgements were suspended and qualified. Even the peppery Bill O'Reilly, always on the *qui vive* for slow-bowling talent, nodded approval: notwithstanding that the youth was 'built on lavish lines', he thought that 'tons of easy pickings' awaited him. Finally, in an act of subtle atonement on the academy's part, Warne was invited back in April 1992 by its new coach, Jenner's erstwhile teammate Rod Marsh, to prepare for the winter's trip to Sri Lanka. It must have seemed to Warne that he could do as he pleased, and be allowed for. Jenner, with whom Warne stayed in his small apartment, decided at the end of the week on a bit of tough love.

I'd decided to give him the big talk before he went back to Melbourne. He came in with a slab of beer under one arm and with a bottle of Limestone Ridge red and a bottle of St George's red under the other. He asked which bottle I'd prefer. He intended giving the other to Rodney as a token of appreciation for Rod's efforts . . . The carton of beer remained unopened in my little place in Campbelltown and Shane said, 'Are we going to have a beer?'

'No, we are not going to have a beer.'

'What's wrong?'

I said, 'I'm angry, Shane,' and launched into my speech, telling him how he hadn't made the necessary sacrifices to be playing for Australia. I did not want him to make the mistakes I did. There wasn't a decent wrist spinner, under 35, good enough to be playing. I wanted him to go home, put his head down and really see how good his best was.

He knew I understood exactly what he was going through. We were so alike in so many ways. Needing to be liked was high on the list.

He looked thoughtful and said, 'You wouldn't want me to lie would you?'

'No I wouldn't, Shane.'

'Well, I can't promise I'm going to go home and do something about it.'

'If you don't, Shane, you might lose some support. A lot of people have faith in you.'

Next morning in the car heading to the airport, not much was being said.

'Do you mind if I light up a cigarette?' he asked.

'Why do you ask, Shane? You've never asked before. You've just lit it up.'

'I won't have one if you don't want me to.'

'Shane, if you want to have a cigarette at 8am, that's your choice. I'd rather you had some breakfast – not because that's what I do, but because it's better for you.'

There I was being a pain in the arse again. He had his cigarette and there was silence again until we hopped out. He thanked me and caught his plane.

It's worth looking at this injunction from both perspectives. For Jenner, Warne was both extraordinary and exasperating. Jenner had had to fight for every one of his Test caps; Warne had made his debut after just seven first-class games. Jenner had regularly been at loggerheads with the administrators of his more censorious times; Warne had been serially pardoned, and generally indulged. For Warne, meanwhile, it must have been one of the first times, if not the first, that an insider in his circle had looked past the charm and bravado on which he levitated through life to seriously question his convictions. The challenge was a meaningful one. Cricket had just gone out of its way for Warne; he had yet to reciprocate its generosity.

Warne has given multiple retellings of that reunion with Jenner in Adelaide; this recent version, published in his own Twitter-inflected patois on his website, is perhaps the best.

Well the next 4-5 hours where [*sic*] life changing – I went to get 2 beers and he said what are you doing? I said as usual a few beers together! He said listen – you are so lucky to be selected to tour again and represent Australia, why don't you get serious, I said like how? I'm working hard!

Rubbish he bellowed out, your [*sic*] fat, drink way to [*sic*] much beer and smoke like a chimney and have never had to sacrifice anything – bit rich I thought coming from TJ as he sucked back a beer and took a massive puff on his cigar!!! Ok then – what do I need to do you think? To start with give up drinking excessively every night, get fit, drop weight and at least look like a sportsman. Wow I thought, cop that! I said ok I will, you wait and see.

Even allowing for the staccato style and the jesting tone, there are two interesting features. First, it is classically cheeky. Jenner is seen drinking and smoking even as he tells Warne not to – the familiar figure of the do-as-I-say-not-as-I-do party-pooper. Second, it is characteristically exaggerated. Warne is seen taking up the challenge, promising that his interlocutor should 'wait and see', whereas in Jenner's frankly more convincing recollection Warne's immediate response is . . . to say that he has no immediate response. As Jenner recalled it, he actually had no idea that Warne had taken his advice to heart for some weeks, when Brigitte Warne rang and said: 'I don't know what you told Shane but it's working.' It would have been more than usually interesting to have been inside Warne's head during those weeks, as he wrestled with whether to pick up Jenner's gauntlet, then resolved to undertake a regime of responsible eating and pounding the pavements round Half Moon Bay. What struck a chord? What drew him on? What made him commit, as he never had, even to something – Australian rules football – that he loved? Perhaps it was a recollection of that earlier failure, of the slap of that rebuke. Perhaps it was a sense that fulfilment lay within his grasp, if he did but reach out and grab it.

Warne's was a blessed and privileged generation, born into social progress, raised amid mass prosperity, basking in unexampled comfort, believing in personal transformation. The cult of the makeover flourished. Gurus of self-help proliferated. Jenner's advice may have resonated partly because of this widespread belief in the charismatic change agent: Warne described Jenner as his 'Dr Phil', after Dr Phil McGraw, the ebullient 'relationship and life strategy expert' who enjoined viewers to 'get real' on *The Oprah Winfrey Show*. It is telling, too, that Warne resolved to demonstrate his renewed personal commitment by the age's simplest and most popular formula: diet and exercise. Warne's career was actually to demonstrate no absolute correlation between weight, fitness and effectiveness: the great impingement on his career was injury, and injury in his case was primarily related to workload. What Warne was doing twenty years ago by eating pasta, shunning alcohol, and winnowing his weight away to eighty-two kilograms was proving, to himself and to others, that his ways were mendable – that he could be serious, that he was worth the trouble. Everyone, of course, loves a reformed sinner. And in Warne's case, they were already half in love anyway.

The pampered party boy was not transformed into the swaggering bigshot overnight: there were times in the following year it might have gone either way. After three days at the Sinhalese Sports Club Ground in Colombo in August 1992, Warne came perhaps as close as he ever did to wondering if he belonged. He had done what they said. He had worked hard. He had slimmed down and smartened up. He had been at all events a model pupil. On the day before the Test, he had thrown himself into fielding training, on a surface that had been top-dressed with highly abrasive ashes that left him bleeding all over his arms and legs. 'For God's sake, Shane,' Simpson pleaded. 'Don't dive any more.' But, Simpson recalled, Warne did: 'He needed to prove a point to me, and I admired and respected that.'

Then it had all gone awry. On a blameless pitch, Warne had been badly mauled by Sri Lanka's batsmen, giving away 107 runs in 22 wicketless overs, as Australia slipped to almost 300 runs in arrears on first innings – a scenario rather typical of Australian fortunes in Asia at the time. In fact, the Test was to prove a water-shed in these fortunes, and remains among our finest cricket fightbacks. On the brink of an inaugural Test victory over

Australia, Sri Lanka panicked and squandered eight for 37 in 17.4 overs to fall 16 runs short, the last three wickets being in hindsight the most significant. Numbers nine, ten and eleven, otherwise unknown to fame, Pramodya Wickramasinghe (to that point four Tests, average 6), Don Anurasiri (nine Tests, average 4.5) and Ranjith Madurasinghe (three Tests, average 4.8), became Warne's second, third and fourth Test wickets in eleven balls, at the very point he had virtually despaired of their coming, the first having cost 346 runs and taken all of 93 overs.

Looking back, what is as significant as the wickets is the fact that Warne bowled at all, at the point where Australia, off the pace for four days, suddenly surged back into calculations. Allan Border is viewed in retrospect as kind of a recession captain, who taught Australia how not to lose as a preparation for their learning to win. Bearded, bristling, ornery, there can have been few cricketers so disposed to thinking negatively. Greg Chappell said that Border was the worst watcher of cricket he ever shared a dressing room with, constantly lamenting the conditions, compulsively overestimating the opposition, preparing always for the worst, because that somehow extracted his best. As a captain he was not such so much defensive by instinct as by experience. Like a child of the Depression who knew what it was like to eat rabbit every night, he carried traumatic memories of opportunities lost – of Botham, of Richards, of Hadlee, of Miandad. Every so often, though, he gave a glimpse of a more expansive spirit; he became like the Depression grandparent who used teabags twice, but nonetheless liked to put fifty dollars on the nose in the Melbourne Cup. It was Border who in 1986 in

Madras threw the second Tied Test open with a declaration over-night on the fourth day; it was Border who gambled his wicket at Leeds in 1989 to seize the initiative from England in what looked like a tightly contested Test that commenced a series walkover. Now, at the clutch moment at SSC, with Greg Matthews tossing up his off breaks at one end, he threw Warne the ball at the other. What was Border thinking?

It may be the wrong question. In such situations, good captains feel rather than think. They sense a drift; they get a vibe. Sri Lanka had one specialist batsman remaining. The likely response of the tail would be to try to hold on while runs were eked out at the other end. That being so, the time was ripe to dangle some temptation. But you could think this match situation through a dozen times and come up with a dozen different responses based on a single minor variable. Would Border have turned to the callow Warne had flamboyant Aravinda de Silva been the remain-ing top-order bat rather than dogged Asanka Gurusinha? Would Border have bowled Warne had the game been to resolve a hung series? Or had the game been in Australia? Or had a new ball been due?

Some years later, I had an opportunity to ask Border about his decision. He replied lightly that Warne had not bowled much that day, that he was young, promising and aggressive. Of course, all these were also arguments against bowling Warne. It occurred to me that it was a decision now too late to make sense of – that by the time I was asking, all questions about Warne were medi-ated through his subsequent feats, that everything about Warne by now seemed foreordained, that we could not turn back time to that instant when Warne had a Test analysis of one for 346. It had been the hunch of a moment that could not be recreated, a response to barely perceptible cues: maybe a hint of sharp turn for Matthews, a glance at the scuffed ball, the timidity of a tailender's defensive crouch, or an appraisal of Warne's own body language . . . and maybe, just maybe, a deep-buried yearning to speculate.

It's intriguing that Warne touched off this response in his dourest captain some way before he had given any solid empirical verification of his talent at the top level, foreshadowing the effect that he would have on Australian teams for much of the next fifteen years: the sense when he was bowling that anything might happen and no plight was irredeemable; the feeling when he was around that everyone was slightly younger and freer.

Three tailenders: it was not much, even in the circumstances. But on imagination reality was now steadily converging. After Warne *did not* play in the opening Test of the Australian summer at the Gabba and thus failed to polish the West Indies off on the last day, Border opined that he had missed the leg spinner's services – a considerable compliment. When Warne *did* play in the Boxing Day Test of 1992, and *did* roll through the West Indies on the last day, it felt a little like a feat foretold – a little like, in fact, *cricket found him*. Minutes before lunch, Warne bowled the West Indian captain Richie Richardson with an almost sub-terranean flipper – the ball Jack Potter had taught Warne at the academy. The rest took less than an hour – the kind of rout Bill O'Reilly had foreseen. Warne's guest at the game had been his new girlfriend, Simone Callahan – by the time he proposed marriage to her, on a visit to the Lake District in the second week of June 1993, he was just about the world's most famous cricketer.

'Nothing is so fleeting as sporting achievement, and nothing so lasting as the recollection of it': the historian Greg Dening's aperçu fits few feats more snugly than the Ball of the Century, the leg break with which Warne bowled Mike Gatting at Old Trafford on 4 June 1993. In the annals of the Ashes, perhaps only one other delivery rivals it for fame: the googly with which Eric Hollies ended Donald Bradman's last Test innings at the Oval, snipping off his average at 99.94.

There are certainly factual and folkloric similarities. Both were planted in the legend-rich environment of the Ashes; both involved a triumph of leg spin, the most mercurial of cricket arts; both related directly to its subtleties and varieties. On the eve of the 1948 Oval Test, Hollies bowled in a tour match at Edgbaston against the Australians, thought he deceived Bradman with a googly, then refrained from bowling it again on the off chance he might be picked for England and have need of it. On the eve of the internationals in 1993, Warne bowled in a tour match at Worcester to England's young proto-Bradman, the Zimbabwean Graeme Hick; Border prevailed on him to deploy none of his varieties, then excluded him from the Texaco Trophy matches to further cultivate his air of mystery. England actually never expected Warne to be picked for the Manchester Test, the finger spinner Tim May seeming better suited to its pudding pitch; there was some confirmation of the view when their own off-break bowler Peter Such picked up six wickets in Australia's first innings.

The differences are more obvious. Bradman's dismissal was an end, Warne's wicket a beginning. Bradman's fall was cricket as Great Leveller, Warne's triumph was cricket as Glorious Uncertainty. Both events, nonetheless, are about rising to occasions, and also not quite doing so. Bradman famously came to the wicket amid salaams from both crowd and opponents. Was there a tear, however tiny? Was there a shudder, however faint? Was the lunge not quite as decisive, the bat not quite as straight, the absorption in the task not quite as total as usual? In his famous BBC radio description of Bradman's walk back to the pavilion, John Arlott wondered aloud whether it was possible to 'see the ball clearly, in your last Test in England, on a ground where you've played some of the biggest cricket of your life, where the opposing team have just stood around you and given you three cheers, and the crowd has clapped you all the way to the wicket'; Bradman himself, disinclined to say such a thing lightly, agreed much later that it was a 'pretty emotional occasion'.

Gatting, meanwhile, was an accomplished monsterer of spin, who had carved up lesser Australian leg spinners in Bob Holland and Peter Sleep. Yet the view of his batting partner Graham Gooch was that Gatting fell victim to a split second's indecision. Instead of striding out decisively to connect with the ball on the full toss, as he would have in county cricket, he pushed forward half a step, in recognition of its being the first ball from a new bowler in the First Test of a six-match series. The daze, as Richie Benaud told

BBC viewers, came afterwards: 'Gatting has absolutely no idea what has happened to it. Still doesn't know. He asked [umpire] Kenny Palmer on the way out. Kenny Palmer just gave him the raised eyebrow and a little nod. That's all it needed.'

Warne? He knew no such inhibition. He might have faced the biomechanical challenge of hitting a target nine inches wide, defended by a skilful sentry, with a 149-gram leather-clad sphere rotating counterclockwise from twenty metres in compliance with some thousands of words of statute; he might have been bowling his first Test delivery in a new country, in the biggest series of his life, on a pitch presumed to be unsympathetic, and at a hinge point to boot: England were one for 80 chasing 289. But Warne did not try simply to land it thereabouts; he did not slide the ball out flat to obtain a soothing dot; he surfed the wave of his own adrenaline, and spun as hard as he was able. It was these priceless revs that mattered. The delivery seemed at first to be drifting to leg, a drift that onlookers were conditioned to regard as disappointing, loose, nugatory; in fact, it was this drift as much as the subsequent break that was lethal, sharpening the angle of the deviation, dragging the opponent's weight one way as the ball prepared to dart the other, like a Pelé feint or a Billy Slater dummy.

The Ball of the Century has its own Wikipedia page; its afterglow on YouTube shows no signs of fading; retelling the tale has seen Warne through numberless sportsmen's nights and official functions, everyone wishing to hear the story from his lips. Alas poor Gatting: Ashes-winning captain in Australia, maker of 94 first-class hundreds, mauler of second-rate attacks around the world. Warne reduced him here to the tagline for a sporting in-joke, the straight man in a cricket custard-pie routine. In *Cassell's Diction-ary of Sports Quotations*, the entry for Gatting reads 'see FOOD; LEG SPIN BOWLING; SEX', his role as Warne's mug comple-menting his reputation as a trencherman and his defenestration as England's skipper after a tabloid scandal. Funnily enough, the same three subject headings would not have ill suited an entry on Warne. Kismet?

'The art of fiction is dead. Reality has strangled invention': so wrote Red Smith in 1951 after Bobby Thomson's 'shot heard round the world'. With Warne's leg break heard round the world, so he first gave onlookers the feeling that he inhabited a different realm of possibility. Rationally, we shrink from the idea of predestination, that cricket found Warne, that fate decreed his rise, that his deeds were meant to be; generally speaking, there are logical explanations for all his accomplishments. Yet in brooding on some episodes in his career – so exquisite, so unenhanceable – even the soberest reason begins to doubt itself. Think about Warne for a while, in other words, and you actually begin to think a little like him.

TWO

THE ART OF WARNE

EIGHT PACES: that's all it was. And only the last few counted. Shane Warne's bowling action was seen more than 50 000 times in international cricket. Yet it never ceased to beguile and excite – that something so simple, so brief, and so artless could cause so much perplexity at the other end, and such anticipation among observers. Once the action coalesced, furthermore, it changed relatively little, even as Warne the bowler changed; rather, the emphasis was on keeping it in working order.

The pageant of Warne started not with the approach, as it does for most bowlers, but with the walk back. This commenced with an unconscious but unvarying rubbing of the right hand in the disturbed dirt of the popping crease – for grip, for feel, and for the reassurance, perhaps, of the ritual. Warne would hardly have known, but it harked back to an ancient custom: until the 1930s, when the practice was finally stamped out by determined application of the law, it was common for Australian bowlers to avail themselves of a powdered resin, enhancing their hold on the ball. Whether it did anything of the kind for Warne is doubtful, but it was a routine that hardly varied, one of those it is difficult to remember starting, and impossible to recall changing. And somehow, as in everything Warne did, it seemed to signify something larger: as dust and grit over time transmitted itself to Warne's clothing, he appeared to acquire an earthiness, an affinity with the conditions. No player is so dependent on the turf on which the game is played as the spinner; it can make, break, enfang or defang him. So although Warne bowled better in a greater variety of ecosystems than almost any other comparable cricketer, his caress of the crease always felt like an act of obeisance, of propitiation of the cricket gods.

Then there was that easy, relaxed saunter to his bowling disc. It was the stroll of a man without a care in the world, whether he'd just beaten the outside edge or been hit for six – as Warne would say cheerfully: 'No matter how far they hit it, the ball always comes back.' Once, at Trent Bridge, he observed England's Robert Croft looking at a big screen admiring a six he had just hit. 'Hey Crofty!' he called out. 'Don't worry, mate. You'll be able to see the replay again in a couple of minutes.' He was right. On another occasion, at Basin Reserve, he delivered a long hop that was hit for four by New Zealand's Andrew Jones, and winked at umpire Steve Dunne on his way back. 'He thinks he can pick me,' Warne joked confidentially. After three orthodox leg breaks, Warne flashed the umpire another smile. 'This is it,' he said. So it was: when a faster, flatter delivery hit Jones in front of middle a foot off the ground, Dunne upheld the plumbest of lbws.

Other bowlers have returned to their marks in a signature fashion. Dennis Lillee used to walk back staring rigidly ahead, absorbed in his own thoughts, flicking the sweat from his brow with a single finger, reflexively raising his arm to receive the ball as he neared the top of his run. For Warne, the walk back was a social occasion. If it wasn't the umpire, it was the captain, a fielder or an opponent. Anything to add a little spice to the contest, a little theatre to the event, to enhance the sense of ease, command and imminent opportunity. All the while, Warne would also be unconsciously rolling the ball from his right hand into his left, savouring the physical sensations of imparting and experiencing spin, the muscle and metacarpal memory. Most spinners do something similar. Muttiah Muralitharan whizzes the ball inside a cupped hand, as though to give nothing away; Daniel Vettori gives the ball an almost neurotically tiny twist, like he is winding it up; Stuart MacGill's trademark is an obsessive gimballing of the wrist, as if to ensure the joint's looseness. Warne rotated the ball from hand to hand languidly, voluptuously, like somebody feeling warm sand run through their fingers. It was as amiable and intimate as a friendly handshake.

As Warne rounded his disc, his demeanour began to change. He did not switch on – Warne was always 'on'. No, he switched the rest of the game off, brought all the activity on the field into himself. There was a pause. It was the best pause cricket has known: pregnant, predatory. It was this pause that Fanny Rush chose to capture for Warne's portrait in the Long Room at Lord's. Warne looks keenly out of the painting – down the wicket, as it were – straight back into the observer's eyes. The gaze is rock-steady. The body is a study in relaxed readiness. The ball is hovering, preparatory to dropping back into his hand. You begin to wonder. What's going on in there? What's next? Most bowlers at the top of their run are thinking about what they might bowl. Warne's pause was as much about letting *you* wonder what he might bowl. To quote one of his best bowling *mots*: 'Part of the art of bowling spin is to make the batsman think something special is happening when it isn't.'

More than any other game, cricket involves a kind of cat-echism – a proposition and a reply. There is the ball the bowler lets go; there is the ball the batsman receives. The same ball to two different batsmen can draw profoundly different responses and consequences; the same ball released from different hands at different stages of a game likewise. Warne let us see this maybe more clearly than any other bowler. There was a leg break, then there was a leg break *from Shane Warne*. To all obvious intents and measurements they might be identical – spin, arc, deviation. But one was simply a delivery, the other increasingly invested with what we might call Warnitude: a cognisance of the science, skill, lore and legend surrounding the bowler.

I am exaggerating here, because nobody has been capable of bowling a leg break like Warne. But what I wish to convey is that the delivery – and indeed the whole introductory choreography – were invested with an additional dimension by the identity of the bowler. What's more, everyone knew it. Batsman after batsman came to the middle determined not to be drawn into the web of Warnitude. They would, they promised themselves, forget the reputation, scorn the aura, play the ball and not the man. Again and again they departed remonstrating with themselves that they would do this *next time*. It seemed unfair, absurd, nearly contrived. Critics carped that Warne got wickets 'because he was Shane Warne'. Warne's response to this would have been: 'Thanks for the compliment.'

While what Warne was thinking during his little pause was secondary to the complexes forming in the batsman's mind, there was, of course, always something. Mike Tyson once said that he visualised his punches coming out the other side of his opponent's head; I used to feel that Warne did something similar as he stood at the end of his approach, looking at the batsman but also past and through them, as though they were already out. 'He gives you the impression that he has already bowled the over to you in his head long before the first delivery comes down,' England's Andrew Strauss said of facing him; it was an impression faithful to reality.

In seeking to articulate how he might have been different to other spinners, Warne has explained that he aimed not for a particular spot on the pitch, but rather imagined the shot he wished the batsman to play. It is an instantly arresting idea, like Wayne Gretzky's famous statement that he skated not to the puck but to where the puck was going to be. You want to run off and do it yourself, visualising a forward stroke for the ball to puncture or a sweep for it to circumnavigate – for anyone other than

Warne, of course, it's tantamount to daydreaming. But perhaps it makes more sense as a philosophy than as an instruction. One of cricket's great bonehead expressions, in the homogenised and pasteurised professional spirit of the times, is 'putting it in the right areas'. 'Right areas' is bad enough: dim, vague and unhelpful. But 'putting'? The phrase sterilises cricket, reducing it to a dumb, static exercise performed by pre-programmed human mechanisms. Where is the batsmen in this? The fielders, the captain, the game? 'Put', bollocks. Warne never 'put' the ball anywhere. He whizzed, whirled, slid, slotted, dangled and darted it. As for 'areas', Warne wanted to dismiss batsmen, not land the ball in a space; this was cricket, not target practice. Jenner put it as well as anyone: 'It's not about where the ball lands. It's about how it gets there.'

Shane Watson has explained how Warne subtly changed his whole attitude to bowling during the Indian Premier League. Watson was rolling his arm over one night for the Rajasthan Royals when captain Warne interrupted. What, Warne asked, was Watson trying to do? Oh, replied Watson, he was just looking to keep things quiet; he may even have said he was trying to 'put it in the right areas'. Watson paraphrases Warne's reply, but you can almost script it yourself: 'Naaaaaaaah, that's no good. How are you trying to *get this guy out*?' To his credit, Watson grasped the difference, and had an insight into his skipper's mentality. If you were not bowling to take wickets, then what was the point? If you were not playing to win at all times, then why were you out there? What is significant about Warne's distinction between throwing the ball up to encourage a particular stroke rather than trying to land it on a favoured spot is not that it provides a formula for Warne-like greatness, but that it illustrates Warne's perception of bowling as a contest of temperaments and techniques rather than an isolated mechanical exercise that might as well be performed in a net on one's own.

The most striking aspect of Warne's approach was its homespun nature. Fast bowlers can often be distinguished by their run-ups; slow bowlers are not so obviously idiosyncratic. But Warne's run-up was nothing of the kind: it was a walk-up, decisive but nonchalant, like somebody sliding up to whisper sedition in your ear. The ball commenced its journey mysteriously in Warne's left hand before being imperceptibly slipped into the right, as though it were being slid around beneath one of three cups by a sidewalk hustler. The right hand then held the ball loosely, as loosely as it could be held without actually falling out.

These heterodox features of his protégé's bowling at first bemused Jenner: he was inclined to encourage Warne to run in faster, seemingly leading to more energy through the crease, and to grip the ball tighter, theoretically imparting more fizz. Warne's preference – as in all aspects of his life – was to do what came naturally. Running too far tired him; holding too tightly made him tense. Jenner sensibly paid heed. As Warne trained and played more, he was able to rely for momentum on the drive of his back leg and the strength of his upper body; that he did not grasp the ball so much as caress it meant that he never suffered from the blisters or calluses that have plagued many a slow bowler. Where his sometime spin partner Tim May literally bled for his craft, Warne whirled away without hindrance.

The action itself was essentially unimprovable. For all the seeming doughiness of his physique, Warne was hugely strong in the shoulders and backside. With only a tiny jump, little higher than it would take to clear a skipping rope, he achieved colossal momentum through the crease, pushing off a back foot lying perfectly parallel with the back line, pivoting on a front foot to deliver the maximum rotation, swinging his right hip powerfully round. There was an audible grunt, and a hint of tongue in the corner of the mouth as the arm came over, but little other semblance of effort. It was almost as though the propulsion came from some external *élan vital*; in pictures of his action, Warne might be a bodysurfer surging through a wave. And while onlookers tended to resist the idea of Warne as an athlete because cricket involves intermittent rather than linear exertion, he achieved at peak energy the paradoxical state that is characteristic of one: immense physicality, seeming weightlessness.

There is no event in cricket quite like the release of a leg break, the combination of the cocked wrist uncoiling to the left and the straightening of the third finger of the hand imparting the ergs of propulsion and anticlockwise rotation. It is a miracle of strength, dexterity and timing. Try it yourself – go on, I dare you. You let go too early. You hold on too long. You get nothing on it. You get too much. Your teammates laugh. Your opponents laugh harder. Hope and humiliation spar. Now watch Warne in super slo-mo, left arm pulling the right arm through, wrist revolving as though on a pivot, fingers undulating over the ball. Observe the trajectory, the delivery hovering for a telling instant above the batsman's line of sight so that his eyes must dart up then down. Check the subtle drift, the so-called Magnus effect, named for the scientist of antiquity who noticed that cannonballs swerved in the air against the direction in which they were rotated. Weigh up all the forces at work: gravity, wind, air density, mass of ball, surface of ball, prominence of seam.

That seam position foretold the tale of each delivery: with the seam pointed to extra cover, the counterclockwise rotation was aimed at sidespin, or the maximum deviation; tilted to third man, the rotation sought overspin, or a little less deviation in return for a little more dip. When the seam pointed at the batsman and the ball was set rotating towards him, the objective was top spin, or a sudden drop at the end of its loop; directed at the batsman but released from under the hand so as to rotate in the other direction, it was the flipper, destined to skid, perchance to sneak beneath the bat. Will it ever be done as well again?

For all the extravagant speculations about his methods, Warne was quite a simple and orthodox bowler. He had the best leg break that has ever been bowled. He had a ball – several, actually – that went straight. And, er, that's about it. There were many shades and iterations between these alternatives – fast, slower, higher, flatter, hugging the stumps, wide on the crease – but Warne was disinclined to overcomplicate what worked so robustly. Once he had his method, his practice regime became about the maintenance of his mechanism rather than the extension of his range. He admired contemporaries like Anil Kumble and Mushtaq Ahmed, but never tried to emulate Kumble's top spin or Mushtaq's googly; his naturally lower arm was the source of his sidespin, and that could not be jeopardised. For how Warne loved the sidespin that made him cricket's big spinning dick.

There *were* original aspects of Warne's bowling – perhaps the most original was the proportion of it directed from round the wicket, into the area outside the leg stump excavated by the footfall of bowlers from the other end. Before Warne, such a method had been deemed either a defensive ploy or a desperate one: Richie Benaud famously turned a Manchester Test on its head on the last day by changing direction and pitching into leg-side footmarks gouged by Fred Trueman. It was a survivor of that match, Bob Simpson, who impressed on Warne the possibilities that coming round the wicket offered, in terms of encouraging batsmen to hit against the spin, or to hazard the sweep. Out of loosened soil, the ball bounces and turns unpredictably; for Warne, the area was a veritable blue touch paper. Opponents would be tempted either to fall in with Warne's tactic or to strain against it: casualties stretched from Graham Gooch at Edgbaston in 1993, bowled behind his pads playing one shot too few, to Kevin Pietersen at Adelaide in 2006, bowled behind his pads playing one shot too many. 'He seemed to attack from all directions,' Bradman said of his mighty contemporary Bill O'Reilly; in Warne's case, this was literally true.

The tactic would have made no sense, however, had it not been for the sheer exactitude of Warne's craft. It was Warne's cardinal virtue of accuracy that made him so threatening from round the wicket, from over the wicket, from anywhere. He could attack a spot on the pitch like a dog worrying a bone. First, perhaps, he might float up something two feet outside leg stump on a good length to pad away. Then he'd pull the length back six inches, and draw the line in six inches. Then he'd pull the length back and draw the line in a little further. It was *that* exact, *that* minute – and, all of a sudden, you were somewhere you didn't want to be, somewhere you did not have control, between wind and water, between hope and prayer. A fascinating aspect of Warne was the number of batsmen he dismissed bowled or lbw in a state of near or total paralysis – padding up, shouldering arms, trying not to play a shot, trying simply to avoid appearing foolish. The victims would seem to have been defeated by the magnitude of the deviation, but the credit belonged as much to the long, steady building of pressure, the gnaw of isolation and indecision that had preceded the wicket.

Midway through his career, like several cricketers, Warne released a video of his great moments – good fun, but somehow not quite reflective of his true art. The last third is simply wicket upon wicket, one indistinguishable helmeted batsman after another, groping, floundering, beaten pointlessly, bowled all over the place. It's exciting, and also meaningless, like a series of whodunits reduced to their denouements, stripped of their sub-plots and red herrings, devoid of drama and suspense. The Ball of the Century became Warne's motif, but it was in its way similarly misleading. Warne didn't just rock up and roll teams over. He niggled and nagged, badgered and bewildered, perplexed and pan-icked – and *then* he struck.

You experienced the sense of gathering danger as Warne's action culminated in almost its best feature of all: the follow-through, as the arm completed its arc and the body its swing, the right boot testifying to the energy of the rip and the pivot by ris-ing above the level of the umpire's waist, the energy sweeping him down the pitch. The eyes would be following the ball all the way to the target, the lips already forming an appeal, the arms prepar-ing to rise. Michael Jordan once threw a full-court pass at the end of an All-Star game which just missed the basket. Asked jokingly afterwards if he had expected it to go in, he replied in deadly earnest: 'I expect them *all* to go in.' Warne did not make so bold; he did not expect a wicket *every* ball. But he expected *something*. Has any bowler in history taken such delight in beating the outside edge? Warne had a whole repertoire of gasps, groans, grins and grimaces to go with it. It was Warne at his most spontaneously joyful, revelling in the chagrin and the schadenfreude of eluding the bat, in the sleight of hand and the sleight of mind. He did not need the wicket immediately; he would have that soon enough. He partook momentarily of the pleasures of art for art's sake: 'Look at me. Look at what I can do.' A *jeu d'esprit* – like picking a man's pocket then giving him his wallet back.

If there should be the whiff of a wicket – what fun, then! An appeal from Warne was more like an invitation. There was a celebration planned, of Warne's triumph, of Australian ascendancy, of the joy of leg spin, of the glee in youthful confidence: come along, bring whom you wish; fun for all the family, ample jubilation to go round. The umpire who denied him was pooping the party. Hey, who brought the boring guy? Few umpires were entirely impervious to Warne's personality, and some were pretty susceptible. Warne celebrating a wicket was a thrilling sight; Warne after being denied a wicket was perhaps even more vivid. He had a repertoire here too. There was a look that said: 'Yeah, might have been just outside. Just outside, was it? Thought so. But we're getting close, right?' There was a look that said: 'You're kidding, right? Phew. Okay, big guy, whatever you say, but . . . y'know, wouldn't want to get a big decision wrong, would you?' *In extremis*, there was a look that almost seethed: 'No? NO? Cripes. I'm just holding it together here, mate, because, fair dinkum, you must be the only bloke in this ground that can't see that was out.' And so forth. If the odd official was taken in, we should not perhaps be surprised. When Warne let loose an appeal, he was offering the umpire a place in his pageant. And such a pageant was it, the temptation to join must have been acute.

I have described Warne's bowling so far by common themes. But not all of the foregoing attributes were present in uniform qualities throughout Warne's twenty years at the top; not all of them needed to be. A time-lapse study of Warne's career, as it were, reveals more features and facets of his bowling, of his cricket and of cricket itself.

For perhaps his first five years, what we might call Warne 1.0 was able to rely on sheer novelty, on his being a myth made flesh – this, at last, was the 'leg spin' about which our elders had told us these many years, and damn if it wasn't just as perplexing as they'd always said. Peter Roebuck once likened young Australians playing English spin in the 1980s to schoolchildren accustomed to calculators suddenly being bombarded with mental arithmetic; English batsmen trying to puzzle Warne out in the 1990s looked like children tackling calculus using their fingers.

In this time, Warne did not so much seem to get batsmen out as defeat them entirely. They would grope sightlessly across their front pads as balls drifted from off stump into a drop zone on middle and leg, where from their perspective the ball seemed almost to dematerialise. Then they'd struggle to cover the deviation, sharp or shallow depending on the seam position, and the bounce, high or low depending on the point of release and the state of the surface. There were, quite simply, no good options. Warne was hard to hit to leg, against the spin; he was hard to hit through the covers, against the drift; you could barely advance down the track because he was so quick through the air; you could hardly cut when he dropped short because of the risk of that wicked flipper; he took wickets from half-volleys and full tosses because he spun the ball so damn much, and because there was so much pressure to despatch the loose delivery when it came. To leg, to off; forward, back; offence, defence – in every direction lay peril.

Around the batsmen, moreover, were arrayed perhaps the best ensemble of close-catching support Australia has put together: Mark Taylor at slip, Boon and the Waughs at bat-pad, with their mutterings and asperities; above all, Ian Healy behind the stumps, with that jeering, jarring soundtrack of 'Bowled, Shane', 'Boooowled, Shane', 'Bowled, Shaaaane'. It was like being cornered in a dark alley by a neighbourhood gang, and having the only escape blocked by the biggest bruiser of all, looming out of the darkness, green and gold knuckledusters gleaming in a distant streetlight.

Such an ascendant could not last, and did not. Batsman began bunkering down; curators began wising up; time marched. Cricket in this country was converging on a twelve-months-of-the-year model. With the West Indies in slow decline, England in abiding toils and India still to monetise its mighty public, Australia's national team was the world's most sought after. In Warne's first five years at the top, he bowled more than 22 000 deliveries for his country and state, and probably at least as many again in the nets, where it is also possible he encountered some of his sternest opposition. Some spinners are loath to wile too long away in training, for reasons both of freshness and of undue familiarity – after all, national teammates often double as local rivals. Warne was at this stage of his career a glutton for work, because it never felt like work, and because if you could get the better of Mark Waugh in practice, then what international opponent could hold terrors for you?

Nonetheless a physical toll was exacted. While he carried all before him in the Ashes of 1994–5, Warne struggled increasingly with a sore shoulder that impaired his follow-through. While he proved irresistible against Pakistan and Sri Lanka in 1995–6, he coped with the workload on the most active of his fingers, the third on his right hand, only by the liberal use of anti-inflammatories, including injections directly into the knuckle. Other injuries also cropped up, as they will in an environment of long days and a hard ball: fractures, bruises, strains and sprains. But it was at the pivotal points of shoulder and spinning finger that deterioration was most marked. Spin bowling is not obviously the most enervating of activities; shuffling in from eight paces, Warne was not outwardly a sportsman in the throes of tumultuous exertion. But this was as much a matter of accountancy as athletics: after years of investment in Warne the asset, depreciation was bound to follow. While surgery and physiotherapy were timed to minimise disruption, what we shall call Warne 2.0, from 1996 to 2002, was a man running hard to stand still.

Between the 1996 and 1999 World Cups, in particular, Warne missed a quarter of Australia's Tests and one-day internationals, and his five-day bowling average blew out by nearly a third. It happened gradually, subtly, stealthily, and the memory of Warne 1.0 kept at bay the heretical notion that Warne was a diminished force; in this time, too, Warne trailed such clouds of controversy, in his public and private lives, that to dwell too deeply on his bowling was to seem almost to be missing the point. During this climacteric, nonetheless, Warne went from being the bowler who did to the bowler who had – a confronting feeling for a man as wedded to the instant and as nourished by attention as Warne. The big leg break, the ball that defined him, proved no longer as attainable nor as inspiriting – and who was he without it?

Warne's first telling of his career, a short book called *My Life Story*, was written in the early stages of his travails; it comes across, as a result, as a little less guarded and more vulnerable than the two subsequent efforts. The possibility that his cricket might not be the same after his first finger surgery in May 1996, said Warne, held negligible appeal: 'I did not want to change into another type of leg spinner. Either I kept bowling like Shane Warne or I'd have to go off and do something else.' Always allowing for Warne's flair for self-dramatisation and a ghostwriter's tendency to hyperbole, this was quite an assertion, aged twenty-six. You'd be pardoned for wondering what that 'something else' was that Warne might have turned his hand to. Merchant banking? Aerospace engineering? Remember: nobody was saying that Warne would not bowl again. Warne was simply recoiling at the prospect of not bowling exactly as he wished.

Common sense tells you that the notion it could be otherwise is fanciful; for all the avowals to perform at 110 per cent, a thousand per cent or a million per cent, most athletes would be happy with a daily average of 90 per cent. But that Warne entertained at this point, however momentarily and superficially, a life beyond cricket, shows how profound was his tactile and sensual attachment to the game. Bowlers talk about the ball 'coming out all right', describing that final millisecond of contact as the delivery leaves their grasp – the pace bowler's sense of the departing seam, the slow bowler's sense of the revs imparted, the general feeling of rhythm and repeatability. Jenner told a flavoursome story of an early stage of Warne's rehabilitation. His protégé bowled a ball that did everything a leg spinner would wish for – spinning, dropping and tearing off at a tangent. But when Jenner opined that it was a good ball, Warne asked plaintively: 'If it was good, why didn't it *feel* good?'

Warne always showed willing. Twice he toured India when more cautious players would have heard their bodies' protests. By early 1998, Warne's shoulder had outstripped the ability of physiotherapy to help; it needed surgery. But he made himself available, only to encounter Sachin Tendulkar at peak prowess – a peak, in his case, of Himalayan scale. Tendulkar prepared for tackling Warne with days of assiduous practice against former colleague Laxman Sivaramakrishnan on wickets prepared to turn and bounce; the only way for Warne to have prepared for his encounter with Tendulkar might have been to bowl on a glass pitch against a wall of steel.

Mark Taylor has made a droll story out of his first experience of deploying Warne against Tendulkar in Chennai. In the first innings, Warne struck at once, Taylor accepting an edge from the Indian's bat when he was 4. In the second innings, naturally enough, he threw the ball to Warne as soon as Tendulkar appeared. Tendulkar smashed a straight boundary. Warne came round the wicket. Tendulkar hit inside out over cover to the boundary. Warne came round the wicket again. Tendulkar hit over mid-wicket into the stands. As they passed in mid-pitch at the over's completion, Taylor was eager to hear what Australia's great champion had in store for India's great champion next. 'Tubs,' said Warne matter-of-factly, 'we're stuffed.' Funny, but only in hindsight: Tendulkar made an unbeaten 155 from 191 balls as the hosts ran out winners by 179 runs. Warne went straight from the end of the tour to an operating table.

When Warne returned to India three years later, the problem was the opposite: he had had too little cricket in the preceding six months, after surgery on his left knee, then a fracture of his precious spinning finger. After a promising start to the series, he was progressively overwhelmed by the conditions then by Rahul Dravid and V.V.S. Laxman, at Eden Gardens. When Australia enforced the follow-on, he and his colleagues bowled on four consecutive days, and deployed nine bowlers, in heat and humidity that dropped fielders to their hands and knees; it was like a nightmare from which it was impossible to awake. Warne at his peak would have found it taxing; Warne off his peak found it as onerous as figures of one for 152 from 34 overs imply.

At the nadir of his fortunes, in the West Indies in 1999, Warne even briefly lost his Test place: an indignity he never forgot, and which we'll discuss in the next chapter. Between times, however, he coped. Indeed, Warne was destined to absorb the attrition of his body perhaps as well as any bowler in history – maturing in a way that outpaced the ability of opponents to adapt to him; maturing as a cricketer, in fact, in a way he rather delayed doing as a man; more of that anon. Peaking: it is an obsession of sports psychology and sports conditioning, although it is also a phenomenon of sports economics. So much professional sport is played, and so unending are its demands, that a standard of uniform excellence is more than the human mechanism can achieve. The best that can be aimed for is maximum proficiency on occasions of prime importance. Succeeding across a full-scale Test series, full of rises and dips, lungings and longueurs, must be one of the most complicated peaking exercises of all. But Warne, setting aside early misgivings, found a way far more often than not.

Because the two dimensions of television tend to exaggerate the grandeur of sideways movement, Warne was a less spectacular sight in the second half of his career; to batsmen, however, he was every bit as demanding and more. The difference between Warne and his great Sri Lankan counterpart Muttiah Muralitharan was once succinctly explained by the Englishman Graham Thorpe as being that while the latter tried to spin every ball with all his might, Warne was constantly varying the torque he imparted. A little more spin here, perhaps with a bit more shoulder rotation; a little less spin there, with the same action but the ball held in the tips of the fingers. Back and forth the fingers twisted, like those of a safecracker toiling at a combination.

While Warne might have played to his reputation as a cavalier, too, he grew ever more roundheaded where runs were concerned. The second half of his career was spent in an environment of improving bat technology, lengthening big hits and truncation of boundaries – a combination that had the tacit approval of administrators anxious about cricket's telegenia, believing it was enhanced by a greater ration of sixes. As he aged, Warne grew more niggardly, more parsimonious, swifter through the air, happy on occasion simply to lay down a creeping barrage outside leg stump from round the wicket, content with a scenario of détente in the knowledge that he would never be the man to crack. He accepted that the lot of the slow bowler was occasionally to be collared, but that did not mean he had to like it, and certainly not to encourage it. His lures to batsmen were not of the 'hang the consequences' sort; rather, they said 'I dare you.'

In even informal situations, Warne gave nothing away. During one late career comeback, he practised at Junction Oval with his old club, St Kilda, as ever under the delighted gaze of a throng of admiring children. When a young Nick Jewell got away with lofting Warne back over his head, the bowler's little cheer squad headed off obligingly in pursuit of the ball. 'Don't worry, kids,' Warne shouted after them. 'I bowled the shit; I'll get the shit.' Giving no quarter was something you had to work at, just like every other faculty.

In Warne's last Test summer, Ian Chappell strapped the pads on for a companionable net session with Warne and Warne's successor Brad Hogg. Hogg affably tossed a few up outside off stump that Chappell was able to cover drive; Warne offered nothing, throwing the ball up only on middle and leg. 'You're allowed to toss them up on off stump as well, you know,' Chappell joked when they were through. 'No way,' said Warne. 'Not after I saw you cover drive Hoggy.'

Warne's evolution meant that he rather bypassed the most historic and exotic of leg spin's variations, assimilated from its English expositor B.J.T. Bosanquet by all Warne's great Australian antecedents: Hordern, Mailey, Grimmett, O'Reilly, Benaud. Warne 1.0 had eschewed the googly in an unconscious homage to Sydney Barnes, who scorned the delivery as unnecessary: 'I never needed it.' Warne 2.0 continued sidestepping it because he was rationing his practice time more assiduously, and there was insufficient opportunity to hone the ball to his own satisfaction. Once in a while he would flourish it, taking his 300th Test wicket with a delectable example, bowling Jacques Kallis through the gate as shadows lengthened across the SCG pitch in January 1998, after setting the South African up with three loopy leg breaks.

But reversing the axis of the wrist and releasing the ball from the back of the hand stressed Warne's hard-ridden shoulder, and required a tighter grip than he preferred; it was actually the only delivery that caused Warne's fingers to blister. Once in a while, a jeremiah would wonder aloud whether a great leg spinner without a lethal googly was not a contradiction in terms; yet Warne's continued aversion to it was a little statement of his own, that he had charge of his bowling, rather than the other way round. 'It's batsmen who worry about variations,' Warne said pragmatically. 'Not bowlers.'

What Warne perfected instead was a slider, released out the front of the hand with the tops of the first two fingers across the seam, and the third imparting a nearly clandestine backspin. It was, in a sense, a family heirloom – Jenner's gift to Warne, as it had been Richie Benaud's gift to Jenner, and originally Doug Ring's gift to Benaud. In Warne's repertoire, it gradually replaced the faster, more dramatic but more physically demanding flipper, and actually became every bit as formidable as that signature leg break. During the first decade of the twenty-first century, a great aura built up around the doosra, the finger spinner's retort to the googly, perfected by Murali and Saqlain Mushtaq, with their India rubber wrists. But Warne's slider was every bit as subversive – a perfect piss-take of a ball. Warne took his reputation as the bowler who had spun the ball as far as probably anyone in history, and turned it on its head, making himself into perhaps history's most skilful bowler of deliveries that either went straight or turned just a little. Make no mistake, Warne could still spin the ball round corners. But the big leg break was now an 'effort ball', and the more conspicuous for being paraded less often, its effect on opponents, commentators and crowds being like that of a shark's dorsal fin breaking the surface and scattering bathers.

While the pattern of dismissals in Warne's career is remarkably uniform, a few variations evince this alteration in method. After the age of thirty, for example, Warne dismissed fewer batsmen bowled, more lbw, the ratio of bowleds to lbws going from from 1:1 to 1:1.42; stumpings as a proportion of his dismissals also declined. Yet you needn't have been aware of such statistical wrinkles to sense different dynamics at work. You saw it all over Warne's face, in his attitudes and in his body language. The bluff, the kidology and air of cultivated knowingness grew with each passing year – the sense that you were watching Shane Warne playing at being

Shane Warne. 'Whenever he came on to bowl, I was like so many people in the crowd,' observed Brett Lee. 'I expected something to happen.'

Warne had always been up for a bit of psychological sparring. He would feign a limp when New Zealand's notoriously injury-prone Chris Cairns came to the wicket; he would address South Africa's Brian McMillan as 'Depardieu', the cricketer's resemblance to the actor being uncanny; he would greet England's Nasser Hussain as 'Saddam', and Graham Gooch as 'Mr Gooch'. At the outset, the banter was more cheeky than sneaky; nor was Warne always in control of his temper. But the older Warne grew, the more his jests and gestures were harnessed to systematic ends. The stroking of the chin, the pursing of the lips, the sardonic half-smile and the conspiratorial wink all added to a sense of imminent breakthrough. His repartee with opponents grew more calculatedly cutting, his ire was ever more effectively channelled. The South African Daryll Cullinan was a favoured stooge. After reading that Cullinan had sought help from a sports psychologist to deal with his feelings of inferiority, Warne bided his time, and greeted the batsman at their next encounter with: 'What colour's the couch, Daryll?'

When Warne wanted an opponent to feel his superiority, he would throw out a bait in two different but broadly similar forms: 'What are you doing out here?' or 'Who do you think you are?' The inference was obvious: the opponent was out of his class, inadequate for the top level. But seldom has a sporting gauntlet been thrown down with more existential resonances. Who *did* the rival think he was, and what *was* he doing there? Didn't he understand? *This* patch was Warne's; by what right did any rival trespass? *This* game was for big boys; who invited the new kid?

In a rare cuss-and-tell interview about his first brush with an Australian team, the South African Graeme Smith recalled Warne's salutation: 'When he walked past me he said: "You fucking cunt, what are you doing here?"' Nasser Hussain recounted a day he toiled hard to make it to 50 only to be beaten outside off by a sharp leg break. He gave an involuntary nod of appreciation. Then he was beaten again. He gave a second nod. As he acknowledged a third good ball, Hussain thought suddenly: 'I shouldn't be doing this. He's going to think I'm taking the piss.' Sure enough, Warne barked back: 'Stop fucking nodding at me. I know it's a good ball. Who do you think you are?'

The essence of spin bowling is to tease and to goad, to incite batsmen to misjudge, overstep, overreach. Warne took it just a little further. He presented his opponent with a narrative. I am better than you, he said; everybody knows this, but circumstances decree that we go through the motions of proving the obvious. I am better than you, he repeated; therefore I dictate the terms of our engagement, bowling my overs at my own pace, moving my fielders as much or as little as I desire, treating you as very nearly an irrelevance, because I have eaten alive better players than you will ever be. Unless, of course, you actually have the nous, the nerve, the cojones, to take me on . . . Warne's 'honeytrap' was what Aravinda de Silva called it, rather nicely. The bait did not even need explicit verbalisation, de Silva explained. It might simply be the act of pushing mid-wicket out two-thirds of the way to an untenanted boundary and throwing the ball up invitingly, with the implied question: Why aren't you trying to hit me over the top? Don't you think you're *good enough*?

There stood Warne at the end of his mark, curling the ball from hand to hand, an action both dainty and menacing, like Ernst Blofeld stroking his white cat. Through his rotations of the ball, he could feel his own empowering properties of spin. Through his unhurried survey of the scene, he could keep the batsman in his crouch that little longer than perhaps was comfortable – time for thought, time for doubt. That pause: it was almost imperceptible, yet time would seem to stand still. It called to mind Paul Keating's parliamentary retort when quizzed by his rival John Hewson as to why he did not call an early election: 'The answer is, mate, I wanna do you slowly.' You might regard Warne in later years, in fact, as exploring that second, more recent definition of 'spin', famously absorbed into the political vernacular of the late twentieth century as meaning to diffuse false impressions and withhold certain information. Warne fell in with that change: at first about deviation, his bowling became more and more obviously about outright deception.

In Australian cricket's green and golden age, one of relatively few ways for journalists to break the monotony of triumph was to speculate about players' longevity. When Australia regained the Ashes for the sixth time in Warne's career, at the end of 2002, there seemed a logical culmination to his career in his imminent 500th Test wicket. Warne was known to have experienced intimations of cricket mortality in 1996 and 1999; he was, in some senses, due another. In fact, the unscripted, unscriptable nature of his career was reiterated, steering him into disaster then back to a climactic triumph, decreeing that he would miss Australia's next fourteen Tests but afterwards enjoy a final three-year efflorescence.

First, Warne suffered a cruel and agonising injury – a dislocated shoulder. Then, he suffered a crippling self-inflicted wound – a dislocated career, brought on by a bizarre drug offence involving a masking agent, the whys and wherefores of which we shall examine in chapter four, which left him in shamed exile from cricket for a full year. In hindsight, the episode is all the Warnes rolled into one: his occasional fatuity and impenitence, his reserves of resilience and stoicism, his capacity to make the best of apparent disaster. Because in losing a year of his wicket-taking prime, he gained several more of rejuvenated physique and drive. Without his rigidly enforced suspension – he was not even allowed to play charity matches – he would hardly have had the physical or psychological impetus to play on. Strenuously denying the ingestion of performance-enhancing drugs, Warne was sentenced to twelve months' performance-enhancing rest – from his point of view, in fact, perhaps the punishment fitted the crime. Warne did not resume, as he might have, a shadow of his former self; he did not play on, as he was perhaps tempted to, simply for the sake of a more formal and orderly farewell. He veritably roared back. In the thirty-eight Tests after his return from purdah, what we'll call Warne 3.0 took 217 Test wickets at 24.75.

Warne resumed cricket in a series that deserves to be far better remembered – by some measures the most extraordinary of his career. During the enforced hiatus in Warne's career, his Sri Lankan counterpart Muralitharan had gone a long way to bridging the statistical gap between them. Cricket's schedules, usually so chaotic, now pitched them into a head-to-head contest at the perfect moment; alas, cricket's television priorities, ostensibly about bringing us all the game's great moments, let them both down, for they went through their paces before a minuscule Sri Lankan audience. Nearly two-thirds of the overs in the series were delivered by slow bowlers on turning wickets against some of the world's best players of spin: Ponting, Martyn, Lehmann, Jayasuriya, Jayawardene, Sangakkara. Each Test lasted five days; each was in doubt until near the end. Murali took 28 wickets at 23, with a strike rate of 45, a performance luminous enough to win most series, except that Warne took 26 wickets at 20, with a strike rate of 38.7, as the visitors came out ahead in three tight contests.

Warne 3.0 was not a postscript, or a postlude, or even a sequel, but a franchise in its own right. Rather than reprise former roles, Warne gladly assumed new ones: he captained an English county, Hampshire, which he yanked from the second division of the County Championship to within a whiff of the title; he visited India as part of a successful side at last, in the second half of 2004; and he visited England as part of a losing one.

In the epic last of these, Warne took on an unanticipated guise: that of the last man standing after a protracted siege, off field and on. As spellbinding as were the feats of hometown hero Andrew Flintoff, it was Warne, 99-per-cent-proof cricketer and 24-carat tabloid gold, who made you look forward to every day's play, and who also kept you titillated about the contents of next morning's papers. You just wanted to be there, see it, feel it, remember every detail. In a profile of Philip Roth in late life, David Remnick of *The New Yorker* likened the novelist's seemingly unstoppable creativity to that 'fleeting period in an athlete's life when the vectors of his physical abilities and his mastery of the game – his experience, intelligence and imagination – meet at the highest point'. That was Warne in his *aestas mirabilis* of 2005: Philip Roth, bowling leg breaks.

It defied prediction. As his countrymen arrived, Warne was in no sort of form, listlessly rolling a round arm over for Hampshire. Just before the series, I watched him compile a first-class hundred on the picturesque little Walker's Oval at Southgate – which was fun. Then, in front of a forlorn handful of spectators, he was unable to bowl a bunch of Middlesex no-names out on the last day – which was bizarre. After invigilating him in the nets at Lord's on the eve of the First Test, Jenner counselled Warne to set his sights low: the way he was bowling, twenty wickets for the series would be a good return. Yet he took twice as many, for less than 20 apiece, towing others along in his testosterone wake, most visibly his 25-year-old Hampshire teammate Kevin Pietersen.

The South African émigré Pietersen, with his bravura strokes, gargantuan stride and sport-striped thatch of hair, was the raciest talent to hit the England team since Ian Botham. Before the Lord's Test, Cricket Australia and the England Cricket Board announced the minting of the Compton-Miller Medal for the outstanding performer in each Ashes series, in honour of the friendly rivalry of Denis Compton and Keith Miller, who of legend competed all day and caroused all night. With a bit more chutzpah and far more bling, Warne and Pietersen were their contemporary incarnations: rivals on field, friends off it, happy in the contest, comfortable with attention, 21st-century glimmer twins, incessant in their mutually admiring glances. Warne loudly backed Pietersen's selection, Pietersen noisily attested Warne's greatness; Warne strove like fury to get his protégé out, Pietersen tried like hell to deny his advocate; Warne knew Pietersen was in that category of players good enough to compete with him, Pietersen was susceptible at the same time to an overanxiety to prove it, and after decisive beginnings growingly tentative.

Not for fifty-two years had an England–Australia series gone to the Oval with the Ashes still in dispute: although an air of imminent thanksgiving pervaded the occasion, Australia could still have retained the trophy with an eleventh-hour win. Warne engulfed the English top order on the first day, including Pietersen; Australia's top order then clicked for the first time in the summer. Twice, England barged and buffeted their way back into the game, whereupon rain left them with the task of batting out the final day. But Pietersen walked into a situation that was, apparently at least, perfectly unsuited to his shit-or-bust ways. From the scoreline three for 67, anything can happen; that day everything did.

Most people forget the precise order of the hectic events that followed. To his sixth delivery, from Warne, Pietersen played sketchily forward, and the edge snagged just enough of Gilchrist's gauntlet to elude Hayden's hands at slip. To scuttle into double figures, again from Warne, Pietersen pushed to mid-on and charged for a run, scraping home just ahead of a direct hit. Rueful glances were exchanged round the field each time, although not by

Warne; he simply retrieved his sun hat and went to lounge at first slip, breezily confident, visibly talkative. The ball was coming out as in dreams; often an over ahead of events, Warne looked like he had the entire afternoon planned.

But no. In the next over, from Brett Lee, Pietersen went hard at a delivery of driveable length. The snick zoomed to Warne at head height – quickly enough, if not perhaps as instantly as some edges. Warne's hands rose late, closed clumsily, and the rebound came to rest behind Gilchrist. Australia was just 100 runs in arrears; there would have remained six English wickets and 80 overs to bowl. Yet it was the kind of moment in which whole careers flash before cricketers' eyes, for Pietersen promptly played like a man set free, slog-sweeping Warne twice into the terraces against the spin as soon as they were opposed again. Warne winkled out two further wickets before lunch, but somehow his progress had been interrupted, and Pietersen drove, hooked and hoicked his way through the day towards a career-defining innings. Sport's outcomes can be perverse. Had Warne snaffled that edge, Pietersen would have been out for 15, ended his debut Ashes summer with an average of 36, and been left to brood on failing at the clutch moment; English fans might have rued their taking Warne at his word about the new man's capabilities. As it was, Pietersen made 158, ended his debut Ashes summer with an average of 52, and proved his mettle under pressure; English fans saw Warne help vindicate his own judgement.

For Warne it was every bit as significant. There was a folk-loric aspect. On his last day as a Test cricketer in England, whom he had introduced himself to with the Ball of the Century, whom he had relieved of 129 wickets in twenty-two Tests, Warne signed off with a kind of Bradman Moment, a tincture of fallibility that, added to events, mixes them into legend. After all, as Joe Liebling said, if Ahab lands the Great White Whale, *Moby Dick* is just another fishing story. Had Warne caught Pietersen at the Oval in 2005, who would remember? As he dropped him, who can forget?

There was a counterfactual component too. Turning thirty-six the next day, Warne confessed to experiencing sensations of completion, contemplating the Ashes rematch scheduled in Australia eighteen months hence, while conceding wistfully that he might not be there: 'If I'm not, I'm not, cricket will move on.' In the end it was Ashes defeat that imbued Warne with the nec-essary sense of mission to see out a further two home summers; had Warne caught Pietersen and Australia squared the series that day at the Oval, there would almost certainly have been no sequel to their duel at Adelaide Oval in December 2006.

For four days of this Second Test of 2006–7, Australia and England jockeyed for position until the last-day scenario was nearly identical to that of sixteen months earlier. England, nine wickets remaining and just ahead, needed to bat time for a draw. Warne had so far been stymied, and left with first-innings fig-ures of one for 167; Pietersen had already made his 158. They were again destined to have it out at the crossroads of the match, and Warne knew it. For one last time, an Australian team basked in the warmth of his relentless positive thinking. Through the Australian warm-ups, teammates have recounted, he was ebullient, garrulous, talking a blue streak about the chance of victory, opening their minds to its possibility; in Adam Gilchrist's words, he 'dragged everyone with his total belief'. It made little sense: in 352 overs bowled so far, seventeen wickets had been spaced over 1123 runs. But rather like the saturnine Fred Spofforth in the inaugural Ashes Test at the Oval in 1882, Warne convinced his comrades that 'this thing can be done'. Then, also like Spofforth, he did a good deal of the thing himself.

This was Warne 3.0 *in excelsis*, residual skill harnessed to latter-day artfulness enhanced by irrepressible confidence. He cajoled umpire Steve Bucknor into giving a lousy decision against Andrew Strauss. He baffled England's Ian Bell with taunts about his alleged likeness to 'the Sherminator'. Above all, he got the better of Pietersen, who started in his usual skittish fashion, almost running himself out, but this time did not survive. Through the first innings, the batsman had thrust a disdainful pad at Warne's deliveries from round the wicket. Come another day, it was almost as though he could not bear further self-denial; spotting a gap Warne had left behind square leg, he committed himself to sweep . . . fatally.

Of all the accomplishments in Warne's career, master-minding this win may be the most remarkable. It was cricket of pure personality. His figures of four for 54 looked merely tidy in the scorebook, yet nobody disputed that the victory was his. Even simply watching Australia go about its helter-skelter chase, Gilchrist observed, Warne's ebullience bordered on the radioactive: 'Warne normally sat out the back watching the game on TV, probably because he was sick of the cameras, but this time he was out in the viewing area, the life of the group. He knew the role he'd played that day, and as we got closer he was saying: "If we get this, it'll be the best win I've been involved in." That was amazing. After 140 Tests he was saying that! It gave everyone a fantastic feeling.' *A fantastic feeling* – that's what Warne would have thought his cricket was all about.

It wasn't over; it isn't yet, quite. There was a Warne 4.0. Nine months after he took his exit from international cricket, 39-year-old Warne placed himself on the auction block for the first Indian Premier League. In January 2008, he was acquired for a knockdown $US450 000 by the Jaipur-based franchise, the Rajasthan Royals. His four seasons as captain-coach was an unexpected career coda. The Twenty20 format was hardly his speciality: he had played precisely two games for Hampshire. Nor had India been a happy hunting ground: his wickets there had been costly and his affinity with the culture far from obvious. Yet therein, perhaps, lay the appeal to him, and also of him. He took a chance, for which Warne was always up. He stood out, which Warne never failed to enjoy. To a competition that could easily have looked parochial, he brought a brazen, blond, foreign flash.

Spinners weren't expected to influence the IPL overmuch; the boundaries were too short and the bats too powerful. But the restricted format turned out to suit them. T20's zero-tolerance policy towards wides compelled Warne to bowl as perhaps he always should have on the subcontinent: straighter, and within tighter lines. The maximum allowance of twenty-four legal deliveries also magnified the potential significance of the brilliant individual delivery that was still well and truly within Warne's capabilities. Hitting consecutive sixes to lead the Royals to victory against the Deccan Chargers, he started a run of twelve wins in fourteen matches, speeding his franchise to an unexpected first-season triumph. No sooner had he completed the last of his Royals engagements than he was signing on to represent the Melbourne Stars in Australia's inaugural Big Bash League. To the question of whether he should play on, he kept retorting with the question of why should he not? His comeback match against the Sydney Thunder at the MCG in December 2011 generated the biggest pay-TV audience Australian cricket had ever attracted.

When the Stars met the Brisbane Heat three nights later at the Gabba, the occasion was just right. The ground had sold out in advance. Warne's presence was milked for every moment, his image alternating on the big screen with his family's, Warne bringing boos and his fiancée Elizabeth Hurley cheers from the crowd of 29 241. As the strains of the theme from *Star Wars* wafted round the Gabba, Warne came on for the eighth over and bowled six slow, teasing deliveries to New Zealander Brendon McCullum and Queenslander Peter Forrest, yielding just four runs. To the first ball of the tenth over, McCullum then came down the wicket to hit inside out over cover, came up short of the pitch of the ball and miscued into space on the off side.

All the while, his former teammate turned Fox Sports commentator Brendon Julian was in his ear, talking to him through a portable headset: when McCullum next settled over his bat, Julian asked Warne to let viewers into his thinking. 'Might be trying to shape to sweep one after that first one, or maybe even go inside out again a bit harder,' said Warne confidentially. 'So I might try and slide one in there . . . fast.' The ball was quicker, flatter, delivered stump-to-stump; seeking to sweep fine and rotate the strike, McCullum was defeated by the few extra ks per hour and bowled behind his legs.

Uproar: the cameras picked out Warne's family party clapping; through Warne's mic could be heard teammates flocking to celebrate. 'That worked pretty well,' said Julian. 'Yeah, not bad, BJ,' Warne replied nonchalantly. And it wasn't, even if in cricket terms it was not so obviously great. Indeed, it was, in one sense, a pretty standard response to a batsman trying to free his arms to hit to off or leg. It was, nonetheless, a brilliant moment of television; it also flashed round the world, thanks to ESPN Star Sports, and to the mysterious personages who rejoice in uploading clips to YouTube.

The print media rather strained to do the event justice. The problematic point was that if you were watching the game at the Gabba, you knew nothing of Warne's wiles; you simply saw McCullum being bowled. The point went unmade: instead, reporters took the fifty-year-old advice of the editor in *The Man Who Shot Liberty Valance* that 'when the legend becomes fact, print the legend'. The *Daily Telegraph*'s account, for example, read like a cross between a film treatment and an advertisement for Fox Sports.

THE *Star Wars* theme song blared when Shane Warne strode
to the bowling crease and cricket's cagey magic man then
proved he could read the stars himself.

In an audacious piece of pre-meditation which only he would be bold enough to conjure, Warne cheekily predicted how he would dismiss Brisbane Heat's globetrotting batting star Brendon McCullum last night.

'He might try to sweep me, so I'll just slide one through,' a miked-up Warne told cricket fans watching on Fox Sports.

Seconds later, that's exactly what happened as cricket's 42-year-old showman bowled the Kiwi dasher around his legs as Warne's glamour fiancee Liz Hurley flashed a million-dollar smile from a Gabba private box.

Those paying attention the night before would have noticed that the prediction made by the cagey, cheeky, audacious, bold, magic showman had been subtly edited – thereby making Warne appear to have predicted the exact shot, and to have explicitly stated his intention rather than more broadly expressed a desire to 'try'. Not that the *Telegraph* was alone. The quote was freely and globally adjusted, by the *Sydney Morning Herald*, by *The Australian*, by London's *Daily Telegraph*, by Auckland's *New Zealand Herald*.

Not surprisingly, the wicket got a big bash on the Big Bash League's website: 'Brendon McCullum became the latest victim in Shane Warne's ever-expanding reel of highlights on Tuesday night at the Gabba, but the mega-star wasn't going to feel too down after being beaten to the punch by an "oracle" and a "genius".' But there was a lot of hyperbole around: the Indian website Cricinfo likened it to the experience of listening 'to Michelangelo talk as he painted the Sistine Chapel'.

Warne? He didn't have to do very much at all. As he said afterwards, bowlers made such plans all the time: occasionally they came off, mostly they did not. On the night itself, he walked back to his mark again and stood awaiting the next batsman, ready to stroll in those eight easy paces.

THREE

THE MEN OF WARNE

ALAN CROMPTON, a former chairman of the Australian Cricket Board who managed several of Shane Warne's early tours, once described his impact in terms of the dressing room *mise en scène*. Wherever Australia went in those days, Crompton observed, it was around Warne's corner of the dressing room that activity seemed to concentrate: teammates hovered, visitors descended, noise and laughter emanated. Crompton said that no other Australian player in his long experience had quite the same effect, except perhaps Rod Marsh, another cricketer's cricketer who, coincidentally, also missed out on captaining Australia despite having all the credentials for doing so.

With Warne around, life on the road was always fun, often a bit silly, and strewn with miniature dramas when it wasn't interspersed with major ones. To sum playing with Warne up, Ian Healy lightly fictionalised a story about Warne coming to him one day and complaining that thirty-eight of the fifty pairs of socks he had brought on a tour had been 'stolen'. Healy did the mathematics:

Mate, you know you always exaggerate about what you say you have. In fact, you basically double your possessions. So you didn't begin the tour with fifty pairs, it was actually only twenty-five pairs. Next, I know you. To indicate that you only have twelve pairs of socks left, you really have twenty-four pairs left, because you like to increase the drama by at least fifty per cent. So actually, mate, the truth of the story is, you brought twenty-five pairs of socks. You still have twenty-four in your possession. So we are talking about one pair of socks that have gone missing! And I'm sure we'll find them in your room somewhere . . .

I know you: indeed, Healy did. And in no other sporting pursuit, I fancy, do players come to know one another quite so well as in cricket, the most protracted, most intermittent, most ceremonial of games. Mike Brearley once likened a cricket team on tour to a family of the Victorian age, proverbially the maker of its own entertainment. Now that international teams are almost permanently on the road, that is a lot of interaction and mutual amusement for young men promoted chiefly for their physical prowess. The off-field milieu, furthermore, mirrors cricket's extreme on-field interdependence, where players are intensely accountable for themselves by that most public of statistical yardsticks, the scoreboard, yet can achieve nothing without the collaboration of captains, fielders and batting partners.

On the field, of course, Warne the wag and Warne the wastrel became something like Warne the wonder, truest of believers, who never saw a cause as lost, who never let a sleeping match lie. What was it like to play alongside him? Cricket having been described as a team game for individuals, and also a solo game in a collective setting, the place to turn after considering Warne the virtuoso is to evaluating Warne in relation to his Australian unit – the most consistently successful in cricket history. A cricket team is a dynamic system operating in changing circumstances. In theory, everyone both enjoys the opportunity to excel and runs the risk of failing, according to absolute and relative benchmarks. The variances are as wide as in any game: there are great players in weak sides, consistent players in unpredictable sides, mercurial players in steady sides. Warne belongs to perhaps the smallest subgroup of all: the great player in a great side.

But even he was to be studied by reference to his fellows, and in this chapter I'll look at him through the aperture of his relations with four other pivotal personalities of his era: Glenn McGrath, Stuart MacGill, Steve Waugh and John Buchanan. Apologies in advance: there will be some statistics. During Warne's career, the game fell into a tedious thrall to figures. But Warne had, to invoke Paul Keating again, 'a great set of numbers', and on some aspects of his game they do shed light. The shade we can add ourselves.

*

Warne and McGrath. McGrath and Warne. Warnanmagrah. Has a bowling partnership ever interpenetrated so extensively? For a decade, they were something like an incantation. Other countries had great elisions: Ambrozanwalsh, Donaldanpollock, Wasimanwaqar. But Warnanmagrah were the great conversation stopper. You looked up and down Australia and its opponent on any given day, and there often seemed not much to choose between them on paper. Then you came to Warnanmagrah. They played for Australia, and they were matchless.

They were *sui generis* too. Cricket has been replete with great bowling partnerships, but they have always been like-to-like: pace on pace (Lillee and Thomson, Hall and Griffith) and spin on spin (Laker and Lock, Grimmett and O'Reilly). Warne and McGrath, slow and fast, spin and seam, were like the Victa Motor Mower in that old advertisement: they mowed wet grass and dry. They covered Australia in all the countries, climates and scenarios thrown up by 104 separate Tests, of which Australia won 71 and lost only 18, taking 1001 wickets between them in that time: Warne 513, McGrath 488. McGrath was on the winning side in 82 of 122 Tests, Warne in 87 of 143: no bowlers with more than 200 wickets have played in a higher proportion of victories.

A perennial issue in their time for other countries was whether to select a fifth bowler. Pitches were flattening, boundaries shortening and rest days dying out. Did you risk weakening your batting by including an additional bowling option? With Warne and McGrath, Australia had two bowlers worth almost any other three in world cricket; its four-man attack seldom looked other than amply sufficient for the tasks set it. And while McGrath's batting was more or less a cipher, Warne's was sufficiently competent to make him a dangerous number eight, obviating the need for an all-rounder.

They were easy to contrast. Beanpole McGrath, meatloaf Warne; rural McGrath, suburban Warne; clinical McGrath, prodigal Warne; McGrath the paceman who nagged away with the patience of a slow bowler, Warne the spinner with the attitude of an express paceman. Their upbringings were a study in comparisons too, McGrath learning to bowl on the dirt track of his family's farm near Narromine in country New South Wales by taking aim at an upturned water trough, while Warne toyed with his gift in leafy Brighton. They were as distinct, in fact, as the vehicles with which each was popularly identified in their early years – Warne as eye-catchingly flash as his hotted-up Cortina, McGrath as self-contained as the Millard caravan in which he lived while working his way through grade ranks at Sutherland CC and as a teller in the Hurstville branch of the State Bank of New South Wales. They were to remain as distinct as their family sorrows, McGrath's definitively tragic, Warne's wholly self-inflicted.

But you can stress these contrasts unduly, for there was a great deal of complementarity to their careers. Both evolved homespun methods, arriving at the right way to do things by experimentation and intuition rather than instruction. There was not really anyone in Australia who bowled like McGrath before McGrath himself, because there had not been a bowler as tall, 195 centimetres, or one as patient, happy simply to hit the seam all day. When McGrath first appeared, Australia preferred its pacemen to fall into one of two types: bullocking bowlers of bouncers designed to counter the West Indies, such as Merv Hughes, or strivers for outswing at speed in the Lillee tradition, such as Craig McDermott. McGrath's virtues, in fact, did not stand out immediately: he was one of those bowlers who wore down critics as he wore down batsmen, by doing it day in, day out, and not just by bowling well, but also by never bowling badly.

In the winter of 1993, McGrath was at the AIS Cricket Academy, perfecting his game by day and watching the Test matches from England by night, in which the first Academy alumnus to graduate to international cricket was excelling. Inspirational? It is hard to believe that Warne was not. For McGrath as a junior quick finding his way in the Test team, Warne then had other subtly empowering qualities. McGrath was not a tearaway success. His first twenty Test wickets cost 40 runs each. When coach Bob Simpson tried to tutor him in the outswinger, McGrath went backwards, losing his pace and his preferment. But in the Australian dressing room which McGrath joined, Warne was an exemplar of following one's own lights, of using a coach as a consultant rather than as an instructor. Whether it is significant or not, the tour on which McGrath made his first impact, to the West Indies in 1995, was a tour on which Simpson was confined to hospital for three weeks by a blood clot in his leg – perhaps a little bit of licence was what it took for the boy bowler to become a man.

If the rise of Warne in some sense prefigured the rise of McGrath, the McGrath premiership was to affect the Warne supremacy. They did not obviously overlap in their capabilities. Warne never jeopardised McGrath's custody of the new ball, McGrath never threatened Warne's proprietorship of the old;

McGrath would usually want one end, Warne generally the other, McGrath's footmarks providing something into which Warne could bowl, Warne's stamina sparing McGrath too much hackwork. But as great bowlers ought, they always wanted to be bowling, and were expert at finding reasons to do so. 'If it seams, it spins' was a Warne nostrum; that is, a pitch that looks conducive to fast bowling will also assist slow bowling, the extra grass providing purchase and preserving the stitches for optimum grip. But McGrath was so adept at dropping a back-spinning seam from height on a perfect length that he could argue the contrary: if it spins, it seams. Once McGrath began fulfilling his potential, Warne never again had automatic primacy in the Australian attack, a transition that coincided with his first sufferings from the travails of wear and tear. Warne became like the favourite son suddenly joined by a kid brother jostling for attention; and the kid brother, he had to admit, had a bit going for him.

The coexistence of Warne and McGrath in the Australian teams of the nineties and noughties is a nearly perfect realtime case study of the dynamics of a bowling line-up. To opponents, of course, they represented cricket's supreme challenge, one, other or both being a threat in all conditions, seldom giving away more than 3 runs an over even when they were not regularly breaking through. To other bowlers, they were ideal counterparts, forcing batsmen to take chances, allowing the laying of their own plans because those at the other end were so explicit and exacting. To their own batsmen they served up readily attainable totals for overcoming, which had the effect of building calm and inculcating confidence. To each other . . . well, that was a little more complicated.

Batting and bowling have different political economies. In theory there are no limits on the number of runs a team can make; in practice there are only twenty opposition wickets to divvy up. Batsmen are always pushing towards infinity; bowlers must essentially carve the same spoils. A vogueish cricket idiom is 'bowling in partnerships'. It is meant to instil in a bowlers a notion of responsibility to the whole, and a sense of reciprocity with the bowler at the other end, but it isn't much more than a fancy way of encouraging accuracy and economy. Partnerships between bowlers are not the same as partnerships between batsmen: they are not recorded statistically; they involve both collaboration *and* rivalry, participation *and* competition; they are, in a sense, zero-sum games. Yes, it's meant to be all about the team, and yes, it is . . . but only up to a certain point.

To illustrate, Shane Warne's portrait hangs at Lord's, but his name is missing from the honour boards that record Test-match bags of five wickets. Why? Because Glenn McGrath – tall, precise, and inclined to bring the ball back off the pitch into right-handers – was gifted by nature to exploit the ground's famous side-to-side slope. In Warne's first Test at cricket's sanctum sanctorum, in 1993, *before* McGrath's debut, he took match figures of eight for 159 from 83.5 overs; yet in three more Tests at the same venue, he bowled only another 73 overs, taking 11 wickets at 19.5, because McGrath bowled 120 overs, taking 26 wickets at 11.5. In other words, Warne missed out on bowling in helpful conditions because they were *more* helpful to McGrath.

This applied more generally, too, and in quite obvious ways, such as in the choice of innings on winning the toss. With the star leg spinner at peak effectiveness, Allan Border and Mark Taylor believed unstintingly in batting first, in order that Warne bowl last on wickets at their dustiest. With Warne's slight waning, and McGrath's irrepressible waxing, their successor Steve Waugh was not averse to inserting opponents to take advantage of early movement: with Warne in the side, he did it seven times, more than Border (once), Taylor (thrice) and Ponting (twice) between them, limiting Warne to eleven fourth innings in thirty-eight Tests. McGrath's incentive offer was Warne's forgone opportunity. Warne's capacity to spook worked in McGrath's favour too. In July 1997, England took fright at the crumbling pitch prepared for a Headingley Test and swapped it at the last moment for something juicier on which seamers took every wicket bar one. In October 1999, Zimbabwe's Alistair Campbell took first innings on a greentop at Harare because he was apprehensive about his team having to bat last against Warne: the seamers again made the most of their good fortune.

Bowlers value individual success, and the Australians in this period were no exception: it was McGrath, after all, who initiated the custom of the bowler holding the ball aloft to accept the crowd's salute when he claimed a fifth wicket, in emulation of the century-scoring batsman acknowledging applause of his feat. The competition might almost have been divisive except for an observable reality: the attack that played together prevailed together. Warne without McGrath had a theoretically greater chance of taking wickets, but a lesser probability of being part of victory. Warne's win-to-loss ratio with

McGrath in the attack was 4.1:1; without McGrath, it fell to 1.8:1. For bowlers, then, even great ones, life is complex, the playing field is uneven, and statistics are more indicative than definitive.

One instance of Warne without McGrath was the stuff of instant legend. Australia having rolled over England at Lord's in 2005, Waugh's successor Ricky Ponting was anxious to maintain that momentum at Edgbaston. With rumours around that the pitch had wanted for preparation, he resolved to send his opponents in. A seemingly innocuous incident during Australia's warm-up, when McGrath turned an ankle just hours before the first ball, then posed Ponting a dilemma: to stick with Plan A, placing faith in the pace bowlers at his disposal, or to go with Plan B and back Warne on a wearing wicket. He pursued Plan A. It was, in its way, Australian: positive, confident, decisive. It was, also, mistaken, as England's captain Michael Vaughan grasped.

When I walked out for the toss I was yearning to win it so much it hurt. I saw the wicket – it looked nice and placid – there was a bit of cloud, no McGrath, and I was desperate for us to have first go. When Ponting won my heart sank into the turf because, frankly, I just could not see us winning batting second against Warne. Then Ricky announced that he was going to have a bowl. I could not believe my ears and almost had to stop myself saying, 'You sure, mate?'

The pitch was in excellent order, the murmurings about under-preparation having been emitted by a groundsman notorious for never feeling he had had enough time and favourable enough

Coming attraction,
in action for Australia
in England for the first
time, at Arundel in
1993 *(above left)*

Outfield Adonis, in Test
repose, at Johannesburg
in 1994 *(above right)*

Finding his way with
slow-bowling guru
Terry Jenner in 1999 *(left)*

FOUR CORNERS

Synergy with Glenn McGrath *(above left)*; asymmetry with Stuart MacGill *(above right)*; détente with Steve Waugh *(below left)*; distaste with John Buchanan *(below right)*

THE BEST OF FRENEMIES

Warne drops his brash new friend Kevin Pietersen at the Oval in 2005, turning history one way *(above)*, then bowls him at the Adelaide Oval in 2006, turning it another *(below)*

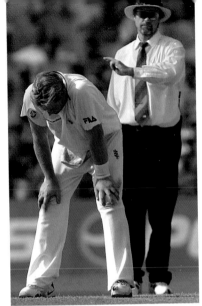

WARNE AT BAY I

Lost in paradise in the West Indies in 1999 *(above left)*

Suffering in purgatory in India in 2001 *(above right)*

Wounded in action at the MCG in 2002 *(right)*

WARNE AT BAY II

Abashed about gambling cash (with Mark Waugh) in 1999 *(above)*;
disgruntled about a diuretic in 2003 *(below)*

WARNE *IN EXCELSIS* I

Checking in with the umpire on the way back *(above left)*; weighing up
his options *(above right)*; the jump *(below left)*; the drive *(below right)*

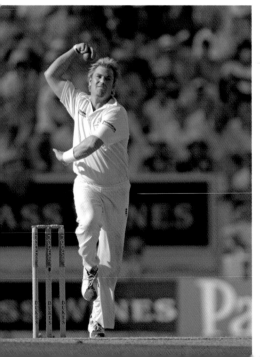

WARNE *IN EXCELSIS* II

Here it comes *(above left)*; there it goes *(above right)*; eyes on the prize *(below left)*; eyes back on the umpire *(below right, top & bottom)*

WARNE IN THE PUBLIC EYE

The bad boy *(above left)*; the loved one *(above right)*; the 24/7 media event, a step ahead of the paparazzi with fiancée Liz Hurley in 2011 *(below)*

conditions. The game went from bad to worse, and only at the end to a little better, albeit to no avail.

The interpretation of Australia's decision to bowl, then, testified to the distorting impact that Warne's participation in events tended to have. For as the Test progressed, and Ponting's call grew more debateable, the *Mail on Sunday* reported a rift in the Australian lute – that Warne had remonstrated with his captain over choice of innings. The story was, of course, dismissed by the Australians as a 'fabrication' and a 'blatant lie', as all such stories are: cricket teams are rather like political parties, in that no member ever publicly acknowledges disagreement.

In time, nonetheless, something like a Rashomon effect became observable. In his diary, Ponting hinted at *some* disagreement: 'I discussed my thinking with senior players including Gilchrist, Justin Langer, Matthew Hayden, and also Darren Lehmann who is working as a commentator during the series, and all of them agreed with the idea of bowling first. Warnie felt we should probably bat if we won the toss, but he could see the logic behind my thoughts.' In his autobiography, Gilchrist denied *any* disagreement: 'I don't remember anybody strongly suggesting we bat. As far as I could tell, the whole thing was fiction.' In *his* autobiography, Hayden described *lots* of disagreement: 'Warnie was livid that we put England in to bat and he did not handle it well. There was a bit of an underground protest over the decision. I saw him out the back of the dressing-rooms soon after and he was very angry . . . Warnie's belligerent state of mind didn't help us. It polarised the team at a sensitive time.'

What's illuminating about this story is not so much the

divergence in recollections, but the assumption into which they fitted, which weighted the issue of loyalty to the commonweal at the expense of the actual cricket question: each speaker had in mind an ideal of unity, which Ponting depicted as being consented to, Gilchrist reported being complied with, and Hayden claimed was violated, betraying in doing so a sensitivity about the power of Warne's personality. For this, it need be said, was a sizeable blue. Not for more than twelve years had an Australian captain won the toss and inserted an opponent without McGrath to exploit the conditions. Rather than optimising their deployment of Warne, the Australians were investing in Brett Lee (back in the Australian team for one Test after an eighteen-month absence), Michael Kasprowicz (back in the team after a six-month absence) and Jason Gillespie (with eight expensive wickets in five preceding Tests); in some respects, Warne's demurral was as much a statement of belief in McGrath as it was an assertion of his own primacy.

It may be significant that the brains trust Ponting describes consulting was composed only of batsmen, and that Australia had no bowling coach on the tour. Whatever the case, there remains a lurking reluctance to acknowledge that on a decision that quite conceivably cost Australia the Ashes, Warne was overruled when he was right. More than seven years after the events, it remains a strange wrinkle in the careers of the protagonists.

That Warne without McGrath was a lesser proposition is, of course, a commonsensical and readily understandable idea. *Of course* McGrath was a great, great bowler; *of course* Warne was enhanced by being a member of a stronger attack. But on looking into another aspect of the ecosystem of Australia's bowling in his era, we find an enigma: that alongside another great, or near great, bowler, Warne was markedly less effective. That was Stuart MacGill.

'Bowling spin can be a lonely business,' Warne once said. 'A lot of the time you are the only spinner in the team.' It was a loneliness Warne did not fight. He was a virtuoso soloist, who needed, and preferred, no accompanist.

If McGrath as a partner was providence's gift to Warne, Stuart MacGill was its prank. Out of Western Australia via New South Wales came a leg-break bowler who at his best was only little less effective, and who was also eighteen months younger. MacGill's 208 Test wickets at 29 would stand out in record books like copperplate were it not for the fact of Warne's 708 at 25 resembling an illuminated manuscript. Their styles were altogether different. Warne's action was side-on and all body; MacGill's action was front-on and all arm. Warne scorned the googly, and nagged at middle and leg; MacGill rejoiced in the googly, and pegged away at middle and off. Warne set his field with care but wasn't fussed about how he looked; MacGill was indifferent to where his fielders were positioned but dressed with care, down to the little apron he hung in his waistband. The personal differences, meanwhile, were as apparent as they were between Warne and McGrath, although somehow less immediately reconcilable. Warne was funny; MacGill was witty. Warne thought of himself as street smart; MacGill was considered to be book smart. Warne had the common touch and simple partialities; MacGill had uncommon tastes and an educated palate.

The real difficulty, though, lay in their nationality. Had MacGill played for another country, he is the kind of opponent Warne would have embraced and acclaimed. Where his slow bowling was concerned, Warne was unabashedly collegial. From Qadir to Graeme Swann, from Paul Strang to Mushtaq Ahmed, he echoed his antecedent Arthur Mailey, who when chided by an Australian administrator for giving advice to an English spinner retorted: 'Spin bowling is an art, and art is international.' Yet Warne and MacGill were both Australians, and therefore coexisted uneasily. Steve Waugh likened them to magnets with opposing fields, shying away when forced together – or at least Warne would, because as the ranking spinner he was regarded as the one limiting MacGill's opportunities.

Certainly on any given day they bowled together, MacGill seldom suffered by comparison. Their most famous dual sortie was in Sydney in January 1999, when Warne returned from a season sidelined by injury to find MacGill the incumbent. The SCG was MacGill's backyard as much as the MCG was Warne's, the initials formed by his Christian names, Stuart Charles Glyndwr, having been selected by his father with a hoped-for destination in mind. Warne struck with his fourth ball, but in 230 further deliveries managed only one wicket more, and that from an undetected no ball; MacGill bowled 242 deliveries for a dozen scalps. It was a little like watching Lock and Laker at Old Trafford in 1956, the former driving himself quietly crazy as the latter picked batsmen off at will.

Everyone was very polite at the end, and agreed that Warne had done jolly well for one who had hardly rolled his arm over in months, but for once Warne might have felt slightly patronised: he was patently underdone and palpably outbowled. Nor was this an isolated incident. In the Tests that Warne and MacGill played together, Warne's 74 wickets cost 30 runs each, and MacGill's 86 cost 21 – a striking disparity. The conviction spread that Warne was sensitive about this phenomenon, and anxious to limit it. 'That the greatest spinner of all time could also be insecure and jealous of the limelight is a lesson in human nature,' wrote the perceptive Malcolm Knox, novelist-cum-cricket-writer extraordinaire.

Yet making sense of this dynamic requires somewhat deeper drilling. Bear in mind whilst evaluating MacGill that the Tests he played as Warne's partner in spin were, by definition, on pitches conducive to slow bowling – and that, given his talent, one would have expected figures rather like those he recorded. It is certainly the case that Warne's existence limited the number of Test matches MacGill played; but it is also the case that Warne's existence increased the proportion of Test matches MacGill played in conditions suiting his talents, and reduced the proportion he played on flatter pitches where only a single spinner was necessary. In other words, while MacGill's opportunities were restricted, his statistical effectiveness was enhanced.

Another way to evaluate the pair, furthermore, is their respective records when they played apart from one another. Here the difference is arrestingly opposite: Warne's wickets cost less than 25 runs each, MacGill's around 33. We're exposed here to an underappreciated level of Warne's greatness. The inference is that Warne was actually rather *more* effective when conditions were, at least in theory, *less* helpful.

Statistics, as I said earlier, seem a sterile measure, particularly of two such artful cricketers, and MacGill on his day exhibited every bit of Warne's star quality – ear-splitting, eye-popping, his leg breaks like wisecracks at batsmen's expense, his wrong'uns as unintelligible as cryptic crosswords. But it's also hard not to enjoy a statistic like the last that confirms the evidence of one's own eyes and corroborates one's own recollections. What always engaged my admiration where Warne was concerned was how well he bowled on pitches that seemed to give spinners precious little assistance, confounding batsmen and also infuriating other spinners. 'He's making me look ordinary!' Phil Tufnell would fume. Terry Jenner used to say that a key measure of the capabilities of any spinner was how able he was to defend himself – that is, how he fared on good batting pitches against batsmen intent on seizing the initiative. This was a strong suit of Warne's, who was as capable of mounting a holding operation as a frontal assault.

One last stat, I promise: Warne's wickets in the first innings of Test matches cost 27.6, and those in the fourth innings 23.1. Compare this to, say, Kumble (34 and 22), Murali (26 and 21), Mushtaq (38 and 20), and for good measure Tufnell (60 and 29). Again, the numbers speak of all-round effectiveness irrespective of conditions. Murali's record, here as in so many respects, beggars belief. But Murali, of course, bowled 57 per cent of his overs on pitches at home tailored to his talents, on which Warne also bowled successfully; Murali was never effective in Australia.

Two of Warne's greatest and least remembered performances were actually in the third innings of Test matches on very good pitches when other bowlers appeared almost powerless. The

Bellerive Oval Test of November 1999 is recalled now for the glorious final day when Australia stormed to victory through the joint willpower of Justin Langer and Adam Gilchrist. It's forgotten that as Pakistan set their hosts a target, Warne bowled 46 overs – 37 of them consecutive and into one of those forbidding winds that seem to arrive in Hobart direct from the Antarctic – to take five for 110. Saeed Anwar seemed unstoppable until Warne whizzed a ball into the footmarks from round the wicket and hit the top of the left-hander's leg stump. The rest of Australia's attack ground out four wickets for 268 from 83 overs.

Warne confided in Waugh just before the Newlands Test of March 2002 that he had twinged a hamstring and wasn't sure how it would stand up to five days of cricket. Yet on days three and four, he became as much a fixture as Table Mountain, claiming six wickets for 161 from no fewer than 70 overs, while the rest of Australia's attack took two wickets for 296 from 92 overs. Taking place in the dead of the Australian night at the end of a long season, it is a performance that has now perhaps blurred into others, even as Warne's hundredth Test match. But I would give it weight as proof that in his ubiquity and versatility, Warne always had MacGill's measure.

Warne also had a ball that MacGill never mastered: the sixth ball. That is, Warne was capable of following five good deliveries with a sixth to close an over out; MacGill exhibited a tendency throughout his career to bowl a loose ball every over or two, a full-toss or long hop that begged to be punished. The two men belonged, in a sense, to two different traditions in Australian wrist spin. Warne bowled in the spirit of Bill O'Reilly, who gave batsmen no quarter, asphyxiating them with his accuracy; in

MacGill could be recognised the attitudes of Arthur Mailey, who late in life claimed never to have bowled a maiden deliberately. In addition to Warne being the more complete bowler, his methods also suited times more rational and attritional.

That still leaves us with the anomaly that on the occasions Warne and MacGill bowled in harness, the seemingly lesser cricketer outdid the greater. How to explain it? Did batsmen play them differently? Did they take fewer chances against Warne because they fancied that MacGill would offer more scoring opportunities? Did the two bowl differently on these occasions? Was Warne inhibited by the presence of MacGill and/or MacGill uplifted by the presence of Warne? Any or all of these are possibilities. Though it is purely conjectural, I suspect that Warne *did* like 'being the man', the go-to guy, when spin was required; there was 'loneliness' involved, but it was of a heroic, me-against-the-odds kind. Pace bowling at the other end probably rather suited him as well, maintaining an unbroken pressure, allowing a slightly longer pause between overs.

I suspect, too, that MacGill benefited from not 'being the man', not because he was any less the aggressor with the ball, but because his methods were inherently more speculative. With Warne exercising his usual constrictions at the other end, MacGill could give free rein to all his varieties. With MacGill providing both a feast for the eye and fruit for the sideboard at the other end, Warne felt perhaps less free to do what came naturally. In other words, MacGill gained more from the presence of Warne than vice versa.

Does this add up to insecurity and jealousy in Warne's case? Discomfort seems a fairer formulation, and I would argue that any cricketer not deployed in what they considered their optimum fashion would have felt the same: had McGrath been demoted to a first-change bowler by the advent of Brett Lee, for example, or Mark Waugh compelled to bat at first-wicket-down. That said, there *was* at least one stretch in Warne's career where that discomfort was acute, took on a darker shade, swept up MacGill, and flecked with bitterness another of the key relationships of Warne's career.

In April 1999, Warne sat down in a meeting room in the Rex Halcyon Cove Resort in Dickenson Bay, on the north-west coast of the island of Antigua, with three figures of his cricket life chief among its influences. Warne never forgot that it was Geoff Marsh who was the first player to make him feel welcome in the Australian team, taking the callow youth out for a drink the night he arrived in Sydney ahead of his Test debut: Marsh was now Australia's coach. Warne's captain in that same Test, Allan Border, was also present: he was now an Australian selector. The figure with whom Warne had most shared history, though, was the new captain, Steve Waugh.

Waugh was the most driven of Australian batsmen, turning ounces of opportunity at numbers five and six into pounds of performance, accumulating runs like compound interest. He was busy carving out a career as batting's great endurer. By the end of his career, millenarians in the American backwoods with basements full of automatic weapons and canned food had nothing to teach him about survival instinct. He and Warne had become fast friends on Warne's first senior tour, the Australia B trip to Zimbabwe in

September 1991. Waugh had then very nearly persuaded Warne to defect to New South Wales, with the promise of better opportunities than in Victoria; they now served together on the executive of the Australian Cricketers' Association. Warne had penned the foreword to the first of Waugh's successful tour diaries, calling him a 'close friend' and 'an inspiration to his teammates'; Waugh had contributed a foreword to Warne's autobiography, describing him as 'just like the average Aussie guy' who was 'humble, unselfish, generous, team-oriented and loyal'. The pair had travelled together endlessly and lived parallel lives: both of them on this tour had wives at home heavily pregnant.

Now their positions were different. Waugh had just come into his estate as skipper, and abruptly found himself under the cosh. Having inherited the Ashes and the Frank Worrell Trophy from his predecessor Mark Taylor just four months earlier, he was on the brink of losing the latter at first try. Australia was approaching the deciding Test at St John's trailing 1–2, and his vice-captain Warne was Waugh's biggest problem.

Since his shoulder had broken down in India a year earlier, Warne had been an unknown quantity, even to himself. He had spent six weeks in a sling after the joint's rebuilding, then six months in rehabilitation, and since returning to Test cricket had taken four wickets for 94 runs each; MacGill in the same period had quietly accumulated 19 wickets at 17. Between times, Australia had won seven consecutive one-day internationals under Warne's captaincy as a locum, perhaps giving him a mistaken impression of his level of match fitness. In fact, his trademark drift had not returned, and he was barely spinning the ball, even out of the rough.

The position of Waugh was little less complicated. He had auditioned long and hard for his role, and casualties had been sustained along the way. He had succeeded to the Test vice-captaincy in March 1997, at the expense of a disgruntled Ian Healy; he had succeeded to the one-day captaincy six months later, at the expense of an unhappy Mark Taylor; this was his first shot at the top job, a role for which the only alternative candidate and some people's preferred choice had been Warne. The West Indies had not been expected to cause Australia so much trouble. They had spent the preceding six months in crisis. The players had held a strike; they had gone under sufferance to South Africa and been belted 5–0, they had been routed for 51 by Waugh's team in Port-of-Spain. Then, somehow, their tempestuous captain Brian Lara, aware that his next false step would almost certainly be his last, essentially won consecutive Tests off his own bat. The Australians then began to struggle instead. Dispossessed as deputy, Ian Healy was wrestling with his motivation. Languishing for want of leadership, younger team members like Matthew Elliott and Greg Blewett were wrestling with their form. None seemed more burdened than the captain.

Mark Taylor had been adept at flushing discontents out where they could be confronted. Waugh, more self-sufficient, more self-contained, lacked the same knack. As he admitted, he had not led a team since the Panania–East Hills under-10s. Not a confident speaker in a group, he liked to put things in writing. Not yet convinced of his authority, he tried imposing explicit plans and rules. He tended to wait to be approached, and felt accordingly 'a distancing of relationships between me and the other players'. One of these players was his vice-captain. As Waugh was to recall:

In Warney as vice-captain, I had a good mate with a sharp cricket mind and a desire to form a strong partnership, but what he sometimes couldn't do was tune into the mood of the side. Often he stayed indoors, avoiding the public due to his enormous popularity, and he didn't eat anything you'd find served at a restaurant, so he didn't spend a lot of time with the guys socially. All this meant that I was left a little unaware of how the team was functioning off the field.

Honesty about Warne's form, meanwhile, was as awkward as discussing a divorce in front of the children. 'This isn't meant to be unkind,' Waugh wrote later, 'but when a great player is for some reason unable to achieve what he's used to achieving, players begin to tread on eggshells around him in an attempt not to make his life harder than it already is.' The eggshells were more brittle than usual for a spectacularly ill-timed attempt to give up smoking, for which Warne was being sponsored by the chemical therapy company Nicorette. But Waugh's field placements during the Third Test in Bridgetown, where he had as many as seven on the fence when Warne bowled, had left little ambiguity about the latter's position in the team, and Marsh agreed.

What can be said about this meeting in Antigua that led to Warne being dropped for the first and only time in his Test career? For one thing, it was the product of an archaic system. While Australian teams for home Tests and for tours were chosen by a national selection panel, of which Border was a member, the time-honoured arrangement persisted by which XIs were chosen *during* tours by captain, vice-captain and a third selector (at the time the coach; formerly a senior player). Border attended the meeting at the Rex not in any official capacity but because he happened to be in the vicinity hosting a package tour group; in fact, his *locus standi* was never entirely clarified because Waugh and Marsh were so adamant in their position. Border was actually equivocal. He sided at first with Waugh and Marsh, changed his mind when he heard Warne speak for himself, then changed his mind back after Warne left the meeting.

Not quite two years earlier in England, the tour selection system had come under strain over captain Taylor's poor batting form. Waugh, having just assumed the vice-captaincy, might then have had the casting vote about his own promotion to the leadership, had Taylor and Marsh disagreed about the former's entitlement to a place; Waugh had publicly opined that the 'selectors at home' should be making the decision. Taylor's stirring hundred amid universal relief had tended to mask the awkwardness of highly paid professional cricketers deliberating on the careers of other highly paid professional cricketers. And the arrangement persisted another thirty months beyond this meeting in Antigua, until Waugh bore the brunt of another contested selection call when he chose to bench Michael Slater for the 2001 Oval Test. Interestingly, in Slater's account it was Warne who was the most sympathetic onlooker:

I felt completely alienated and rejected. Then Shane Warne walked in and put his arm around me. He asked if I was okay and gave me a cigarette. 'Think about what you're doing Slats,' he said. 'Don't do anything that can affect your future.'

Perhaps Warne was looking back wondering how close he had come to doing so. Warne, Waugh reported of the meeting in Antigua, took the decision 'stoically'; for his own part, Waugh 'experienced a heavy weight being lifted'. But this heavy weight had to be put down somewhere, and its displacement was considerable. The aspects of his omission that particularly rankled with Warne are not difficult to imagine. It was not the judgement of a distant body of greybeards, but the verdict of friends and contemporaries. Warne could be dismissive of his elders and critics. What did they know? But he had a strong sense of his status in the eyes of his fellows; he believed in caste and hierarchy. A pet peeve he once shared was young cricketers who, when autographing bats, did so too close to the top: 'You should earn your way up the autograph bat.' He had earned his way up; he now felt that should count for something. Some Australian vice-captains have seen the position as a nominal appointment. Warne never did, and was further aggrieved when Waugh, in discussing Warne's position publicly, depreciated the role's relevance.

Above all, Warne's response to his axing exposed the change he had undergone in the decade. He was in terrible form – the worst of his career. Most cricketers would have comprehended their omission; a proportion would even have welcomed it as a private respite from public failure. Jenner actually urged him not to think of it as being dropped at all: rather, Warne should regard it as a rest following a premature return from injury. Warne could not reconcile himself even to the decision of trusted friends and the counsel of his closest mentor; on the contrary, he railed against it. It was a boorish, peevish, petulant rage; it was egregiously unfair to the medium-pacer Adam Dale and off spinner Colin Miller chosen ahead of him, yet it testified also to how Warne had come to need cricket, the game that had come along and found him those years ago when he hadn't really been looking for it. He wanted to play. He *had* to play. If he wasn't playing, how could he redeem himself? If he wasn't playing, *who was he?*

In his fearlessly frank diary of his last season playing football at Millwall in 1973–4, Eamon Dunphy describes being on the brink of losing his place as a private purgatory – a hell that instilled in him deeper admiration of those great players who somehow fight on in spite of it. There is grandeur, he says, about players who are 'willing to make mistakes when they know how bad they look', and who continue 'wanting the ball' even though every time it arrives 'it is a personal crisis'. They'll endure this purgatory because what lies beyond is the professional death of omission. 'What is real is what goes on the teamsheet,' concludes Dunphy. 'The rest is rubbish.'

That counted doubly so for Warne in his predicament. In his time, the Australian cricket team had almost completely decoupled from the rest of the Australian game. It was no longer a group summonsed every so often from the Australian states to represent the nation; it was a self-reinforcing, almost self-governing unit that travelled the country and the world for most of the year, an elite of elites. It was exclusive in a financial sense, the top echelon of cricketers being the only ones paid as top athletes in other pursuits were accustomed to; it was exclusive in a cultural sense, too, because those expelled from its privileged circle slipped into an ignominious twilight. Warne, of course, had not quite been consigned to the outer darkness. But that in its way was as demoralising, having to face up every day to his reduced station.

After Warne's omission, there was what his roommate Adam Gilchrist called a 'weird vibe' around the Australian team. Warne sulked – there is no other word for it. He went through the motions of the warm-ups each morning of the Test, then adjourned sullenly to the dressing room, in whose toilets he smoked fiercely. In fact, he was shortly to embarrass his sponsors by being caught *in flagrante* with a cigarette at a Bridgetown nightclub called the Boat Yard in the presence of a camera, the resulting photograph ending up on the front page of the *Daily Mail*, then to mortify his administration by putting his name to a column that trashed Sri Lanka's captain Arjuna Ranatunga, which was splashed across *The Times*. These were the risky and provocative behaviours of an angry man. Although Australia won the Antigua Test to save Waugh's blushes, and Warne resumed his place in the subsequent one-day series, Gilchrist found Warne bitter and seething, openly countenancing retirement.

Waugh then arrived in England at the head of his team for the 1999 World Cup to questions almost solely about Warne. Would he play? Would he not? Was he still the great of yore? The issue was inescapable. The team seemed less influenced by Waugh's leadership than by Warne's humours; the captain's attempt to impose a curfew on players obtained a particularly nonplussed response, and was rescinded on the encouragement of Tom Moody, a wise old head on whom Waugh leaned ever increasingly for advice. It was Moody, and also the sport psychologist Sandy Gordon, who reported to Waugh that there was restlessness in his camp, and that Warne was a locus of discontent. Off-key, off-balance, Australia stumbled to the edge of elimination from the tournament's Super Six stage by losing to New Zealand then Pakistan. The published recollections of captain and vice-captain from the time are full of subtle contrasts, reflective of their states of mind. On the night of Australia's defeat by New Zealand, for example, players gathered at an Italian restaurant in Cardiff to mark the birth overnight of Warne's son Jackson. Warne's account suggests a raucous night out: 'We partied as never before . . . The two sides of the long table squared up for competitions in sculling pints of beer and shots of spirits. We even had a singing competition against a group of priests, who had doubtless arrived expecting a quiet, civilized meal.' Waugh remembered it as 'a subdued celebration . . . despite cigars all round'. Glimpsed between unfathomable lows, the old Warne high was suddenly like a whimsicality at a wake.

When the ABC's Tim Lane reported on well-placed whispers that all was not well in the Australian camp, Waugh and Warne indulged in displays of shoulder-to-shoulder unity: following the aforementioned party-political tradition, they could hardly do otherwise. Much later, in his autobiography, Waugh was more candid about his frustrations: 'Warne *was* causing some friction behind the scenes over the captaincy. He was lonely, hurt, annoyed and frustrated, and quite frankly sick of the media attention.' Waugh's efforts to root the problem out, though, were halting and unsuccessful: 'Was there a problem? If so, I needed to confront it and find a solution. When I brought the general issue up of player discontent at the pre-game team meeting, all I got were vacant looks and full support.'

Warne himself might have struggled to explain exactly what

he was feeling. A sense of betrayal? A deep-buried fear? He had been below his best for more than a year. It was a long time to urge himself on, to continue repeating that all would eventually be well, that patience would ultimately be rewarded. He had entertained giving the game away three years earlier because of injury; he experienced similar sensations now, as for every step forward he seemed to take two back. Warne flattered to deceive at Old Trafford, where the West Indies turned timid after the early loss of Lara. But in the Super Six stage, his struggles resumed. India's Ajay Jadeja and Robin Singh hit him for three sixes in an over at the Oval, and Zimbabwe's Neil Johnson for four fours in an over at Lord's. After that game, Warne spoke openly of retirement – only to bowl well at training the next day and seemingly set the thought aside.

Meanwhile Waugh, a reserved, taciturn man who kept himself under close control, was wrestling with his own insecurities. His one-day captaincy was on trial. In eighteen months, Australia had won only half its matches under his leadership; his batting had in that time rather tapered off. The possibility existed that in the event of Australian failure at the Cup, the selectors might turn from Waugh to . . . Warne. The man most conflicted in any unsuccessful team is always the ambitious vice-captain, collective failure in a way serving individual advancement.

At various times in Warne's career, the safest place for him seemed actually to be on the field, when all his energies were channelled into defeating an opponent, rather than diffused among the challenges of worrying about his life, grumbling about his detractors, controlling his temper and subduing his appetites. And by placing his career in his own crude balance, Warne suddenly seemed to achieve clarity. The night before Australia played South Africa at Headingley in the last Super Six game, Warne threw out an observation both tangential and characteristic: that the partiality of South Africa's perky opening batsman Herschelle Gibbs for tossing the ball away after taking a catch was going to get him into trouble one day; it was too lairy, too cute. His teammates cracked up – this from their own king of lairs.

Though the Australians were not to know, the South Africans themselves were worrying about this habit, which had begun spontaneously during a day-night game at the MCG in December 1997, when Gibbs had cast the ball aside after catching Warne because he was in a hurry to get off the ground to go to the toilet. When he'd started doing it compulsively, coaches had tried to discourage him, only to find Gibbs airy and evasive. 'It's just me,' he would say; why shouldn't he have his fun? Sensitive to the nuances of style, and also to the cricketer just a little above and ahead of himself, Warne arrowed in with his ritual questions. What was Gibbs doing out there? And just *who did he think he was*?

In the environment of a team meeting – something that is usually about the drumming in of basics – Warne's remark rather hung in the air. In a dourly disciplined South African line-up, Gibbs was a key figure – a crisp strokemaker, a spring-heeled infielder. Yet here was Warne drawing attention to a weakness that rather cut Gibbs down to size. It was something to think about, to watch out for – a tiny edge, an infinitesimal scrap of reinforcement. It was indicative, too, of a cricketer suddenly focusing on his next contest – putting on his game face, strapping on his battle armour.

When Australia took the field the next morning, Warne was as vocal and vehement as he had previously been subdued and sullen, perhaps suddenly brooding on how he would like to go out, how he would wish to be remembered. Just as Gibbs looked like seizing the game for South Africa, Warne dismissed his perennial victim Daryll Cullinan and opposing captain Hansie Cronje in a crucial over, then took a brilliant, full-length diving catch to arrest the headlong progress of Lance Klusener. Gibbs made a sprightly hundred, but had to pay Warne his tribute, hitting him for only a single boundary in twenty-five deliveries. South Africa's seven for 271 was not the total it had threatened from one for 140.

It appeared enough as Australia slipped to three for 68 after twenty-one overs, but Waugh then seized the day with strokes that smouldered with intensity, and luck that savoured of impunity. For with the job half done, he flicked Klusener waist-high to mid-wicket, where Gibbs, too keen to execute his trademark flick, tossed the catch to one side. Umpire Srinivas Venkataraghaven was of a mind to give Waugh out anyway, but his colleague Peter Willey hesitated, and the benefit of doubt went the Australian captain's way.

The rest is history – mostly, anyway. 'You've just lost the match,' Waugh gloated, a line that by the time it had been improved on by the power of myth had become, 'What does it feel like to drop the World Cup?' Gibbs has always denied hearing any comment. Warne's contribution to the event needed no improving. Here is a difference between the two Australians: Waugh was a canny cricketer, Warne an uncanny one. Has anyone in history ever foreseen not just that a catch would be dropped but *how* it would be dropped? As Australia ransacked 204 from its last 172 deliveries to barge into the semifinals against the same opponent, they could feel themselves favoured by both rational and irrational forces.

Warne then took a blow from a quarter he had not anticipated. In Melbourne, David Hookes, a former Australian vice-captain turned broadcast pundit, volunteered that there were further disclosures in prospect about Warne's tarrying with a bookmaker five years earlier. Hookes had been first to hint of the affair late the previous year, so the remark came with some authority, even if it proved to be without substance. But in taking the gloss off Australia's progress into the semifinals, it cut deeply. Hookes was a semi-legendary figure, a batsman to whom an awestruck Warne had bowled at the Academy, a personality whose autograph had been on the Gray-Nicolls bat Warne owned at the time. Hookes was a familiar, too, of Warne's close friend Ian Chappell – he was, in other words, not a kibitzer whom Warne could lightly dismiss.

In fact, that tore it. During a team recovery session at Hyde Park in central London, Waugh and Warne formed their own Speakers' Corner. Was Waugh a little more confident as a result of his unbeaten hundred at Headingley? Was Warne that little more vulnerable for being, this time at least, an innocent accused? Whatever the case, two cricketers, anxious and brooding in their own different ways, shared their innermost thoughts – or, at any rate, Warne talked and Waugh listened. 'I told Steve that enough was enough,' Warne recalled. 'Plain and simple. In a nutshell, I was ready to quit.' Waugh, thinking Warne at an 'all-time low', asked him not to make any decision hastily. There was at last some candour between them. Warne shared some of his umbrage with Waugh for the way he had minimised the significance of the vice-captaincy: how would Waugh have felt had Taylor said the same of the role when Waugh held it? In general, though, the conversation seems more to have been a talking aloud, with 'the media', as personified here by Hookes, perhaps providing a useful focus for combined ire, an external enemy for which to declare common disdain. And it was a recognition, reinforced by their respective recent performances against South Africa, of mutual need.

Warne continued to make free with his convictions that the end of his career was nigh. After Waugh's last few pre-match remarks before the Edgbaston semifinal, Warne added weightily that this might be 'the last game for Australia for a couple of boys', then repeated it for additional emphasis. It is just possible he had Moody in mind, although the obvious inference was that the comment was autobiographical. There was not much time to digest the remark, but again it hung meaningfully through a day on which it might very easily have come true. Waugh again took control of a languishing innings against a formidable attack, and with Michael Bevan guided Australia to a middling 213, but Gibbs and his partner Gary Kirsten had surged to none for 43 from their first ten overs of the reply when Waugh threw Warne the ball.

Four deliveries in his first over were to the left-handed Kirsten, suggesting turn although no particular bite. The day's earlier cloud cover had lifted, and a noisy corner of the ground staked out by South Africans was celebrating each run; it would take something out of the ordinary to counteract both. It was the kind of moment that cried out for Warne. When he resumed to Gibbs, Warne simply spun as hard as it was still in him, and the leg break swerved to leg before whipsawing to hit the top of off. It differed from the delivery that had done for Mike Gatting six years earlier: bulwark Gatting's first line of defence had been his pad; one-day sprite Gibbs was intent on working it to leg. Both batsmen, however, were equally flummoxed: Gibbs was left standing a foot outside leg stump, as though glued there, and all the way off kept glancing over his shoulder, looking for a big-screen replay. Warne, meanwhile, was in full cry, his exhortations of 'Come on! Come on!' reverberating through the effects microphones.

In his next over, Warne bowled Kirsten through a befuddled sweep and had Cronje caught at slip – off the batsman's boot, although the naked eye was not to tell. A camera panning the players' balcony caught the looks of South Africans almost catatonic with shock; the Australians on the field were as jubilant as under-12s. 'It sums up what Warnie can do to you emotionally,' Adam Gilchrist would say. 'One minute you'd be asking yourself why he was carrying on a certain way. And the next, he was engineering one of the greatest experiences of your cricket life . . . I was frustrated with Warnie for some of that tour, but I also owed him some moments I will never forget.'

They kept coming. The hapless Cullinan ran himself out; there were two more near run-outs in Warne's seventh over; there were seventeen consecutive scoreless deliveries, building almost Hitchcockian suspense. The only dilemma for Waugh was whether to hold back a couple of Warne overs, which he finally elected to do when South Africa was four for 71, with a required run rate of nearly a run a ball. Eight overs, four maidens, three for 12: very seldom can the word 'spell' in cricket have lived up so fully to its dual meanings.

As the South Africans regrouped and the Australians persisted, Warne and Waugh remained conspicuous: Warne was the most voluble figure on the field, maintaining a constant chatter and chi-acking from point then wide mid-on; wintry Waugh stood at cover, solemn and inscrutable. The match slumbered fitfully, awaiting the latter's redeployment of the former. Cheers and jeers competed as Warne resumed with the South Africans needing 61 runs from the last eight overs, an equation he worsened with an over worth a single each to Jacques Kallis and Shaun Pollock. In Warne's last over, Kallis miscued to wide mid-off where an on-rushing Reiffel spilled the catch, Warne emitting an expletive as the ball returned, then perhaps muttering a few silent ones as Pollock lofted a six down the ground and a boundary through cover.

Throwing up his penultimate delivery gamely, however, Warne drew Kallis into a false stroke to cover, where Waugh took the catch. Bowler and catcher converged on each other at walking pace and with the utmost seriousness, as though in mutual recognition that they needed to keep their heads in case all about them lost theirs. Which they did. As Waugh rang changes through the closing overs, Warne's voice pealed with encouragements and urgings above the hubbub, even in the breathless final over when he kept repeating the advice: 'A draw will get us through! A draw will get us through!' That is, in the event of the scores being tied, Australia would advance to the final on net run rate – a final prophecy he did not need to wait long to see fulfilled.

You could write endlessly about this game, by common consent the best one-day international ever played: the electrifying speed of Pollock and Allan Donald, the fielding wizardry of Jonty Rhodes and Mark Waugh, the nerveless poise of Klusener's hitting and the nervous breakdown of his running, the chaotic ballet of its climax, captured in a famous photograph in which Warne is charging towards the shattered stumps as a shattered Donald peels away to collect his dropped bat. But what these back-to-back beatings of South Africa proved to be, quite aside from the hinge point in a World Cup triumph, was a turning point in relations between Warne and Waugh, respectively the most exciting and the most authoritative Australian cricketers of their time. The experience did not restore their former warmth.

Having sunk their differences in order to win, I suspect, they realised that they did not have to like each other in order to succeed. They became 'diametrically allied', to borrow William Safire's description of Richard Nixon and George Meany: 'That is, they respected and admired each other and did not like or trust each other.' As their coexistence continued, Warne could almost be seen as the exception to everything Waugh stood for. Waugh accorded cultish reverence to the baggy green cap; Warne barely wore it. Waugh set enormous store on systematic preparation and set goals; Warne advertised his own preparatory ritual as 'a fag and a cup of tea', then aiming to hit the top of off; uxorious Waugh believed that 'a happy family man was a more contented player who could focus better on his game'; Warne at times seemed to thrive on the chaos of his personal life.

It worked, of course. 'All the successful teams I've played in have been dominated by people willing to see past others' faults and appreciate their strengths,' concludes Waugh in his autobiography – a perspective that can have no other inspiration. For much of the rest of their time together, furthermore, they had a proxy figure through whom they could essentially live their differences out: their coach, John Buchanan.

In surveying the rise of the national coach in cricket, the first cause for wonder is not the quarter-century in which they have been a phenomenon, but the preceding century in which they were not. Every other sport knelt at the altar of the coach, manager or guru; in cricket, despite its technical rigour and complexity, the captain remained all-powerful, and the game was learned without formally being taught. Down Under, coaching was usually identified with a restraint on the flowering of innate ability. 'In Australia, boys learn by watching each other and any grown up cricketers who they see,' wrote Fred Spofforth. 'The result is individuality, and their natural ability is not dwarfed by other people's ideas.'

A hundred years ago, Dr Leslie Poidevin saw cricket as bred in the Australian bone: 'There's something marvellous about a young Australian's devotion to and aptitude for the game. He gets no "coaching". He merely takes a bat and it seems to be "in him" to know what to do with it.'

Part of the legend of giants of the Australian game like Donald Bradman and Bill O'Reilly was their flouting of orthodoxies. O'Reilly recalled being the recipient of coaching advice at the

Sydney Cricket Ground nets within the hearing of Charlie Turner; Turner sidled up and told him to take no notice, confiding that he had profitably ignored coaches' advice all his career. There was certainly no question of a Test team having a full-time coach. If players had something to learn, they did so from one another rather from a formal authority. When Neil Harvey struggled to come to terms with English conditions on his first tour in 1948, he sought advice from Bradman via his roommate Sam Loxton, and received back the oracular counsel: 'Hit the ball on the ground and you can't be caught.'

The *English* believed in correct technique – which was, of course, a justification for Australian difference. Australians rejoice in the joke about the English coach who reprimanded a boy for his grip. 'But sir,' says the boy, 'this is the way Bradman held the bat.' The coach replies: 'Well, just think how many runs he would have made had he held the bat properly.' Not even the English, though, believed in a coach for their Test team. In his managerial role on England's winter tours to India, Pakistan/New Zealand, Australia and the West Indies in the late 1970s and early 1980s, the former Surrey great Ken Barrington combined administrative responsibilities with technical guidance and selection duties. But Barrington took on his tasks because he was Barrington rather than because he was coach, and was not replaced on his death.

Australia's decision to appoint a full-time national coach in March 1986 was thus made in the face of considerable scepticism. The first man offered the job, Ian Chappell, declined because he doubted the role was necessary; the second, Bob Simpson, said he regarded it as a finite appointment, and foresaw making himself redundant. When England appointed Micky Stewart to a similar role later the same year, he was likewise designated not 'coach' but 'team manager'. The impetus for the appointments of Simpson and Stewart was simple: dislocation in leadership following the retirement of senior players. In the preceding five years, Australia had had four captains and England six; the latest appointments, Allan Border and Mike Gatting, were bearing their burdens uneasily. Simpson ascribed the need for his job to the 'diminishing role of the Australian captain and the almost total destruction of peer influence within Australian cricket' after the sudden professionalisation of the game in the wake of Kerry Packer's World Series Cricket.

In an environment of constant comings and goings, the leathery, hard-bitten, hard-driving Simpson became the face of continuity and the personification of perseverance. Yet cricket's doubts remained. Experience playing Test cricket tended to be a minimum prerequisite for coaching it, and even then not all agnostics were disarmed. No admirer of Simpson in any case, Ian Chappell tirelessly expounded the view that players of international quality should need no guidance or additional instruction – a view that struck a chord with the closest player he had to a modern mentee, Warne.

A font of lore and a wellspring of opinion, Chappell is the most charismatic of former Australian captains. He and Warne became properly acquainted when the latter joined Channel Nine in March 1996 and was sent to Augusta to watch its commentary team, including Chappell, call the US Masters. He warmed to Chappell's tales of full-blooded competition and full-bodied socialising, and enjoyed Chappell's capacity for boiling the game down to straightforward nostrums: 'Ian always says that it is a simple game and it is best to keep it as simple as you can. He thinks about the game the way he played – aggressively.' For Chappell, Warne's regard was a confirmation of continued relevance, a reminder of his prime, and a vindication of his era.

A subtle transformation took place. Warne, who had been about everything bright, shiny and new, began regarding himself as a kind of throwback, a 'real' cricketer, of the 'old school', his efforts to play the part of the craggy old pro in the Australian dressing room occasioning some wry glances. Jason Gillespie offered a humorous glimpse of Warne holding court during a Gabba Test when a group of Australian Rules footballers from the Brisbane Lions dropped in:

He decided to grab a beer out of the fridge, sit in his corner, put an ice pack on his knee and have the fags nearby. Maybe he wanted to portray a bit of an 'old school' image to the Brisbane lads. The rest of us all looked at each other and thought to ourselves, What's going on here? Warnie with a beer? We were all having a bit of a giggle, and in came the Lions lads to say 'Hi'.

Nothing was really said until Glenn McGrath walked in. He sat down, noticed Warnie with a frostie and asked, 'What the hell are you doing with a beer?' Warnie replied, 'Bowling day, mate – just finishing the day with a beer.' Glenn responded, 'I've never, ever seen you with a beer.' Warnie came back with, 'Oh, hang on, mate: I always have a beer at the end of a bowling day.' We all pissed ourselves laughing, because none of us had ever seen him have a beer after a bowling day.

For the rest of the summer, Darren Lehmann, Gilly [Adam Gilchrist] and I took it upon ourselves to make sure that at the end of each bowling day, Shane had a beer in his spot in the rooms. We chortled away, thinking we were the funniest blokes in the world. After about six months, he said to me: 'Dizzy, enough is enough, you've made your point – well done.'

Ian Chappell reciprocated, with cameos of his own.

At a Test a few years ago I was waiting to interview the captains at the toss, when Shane came bounding up. 'Why are we doing these stupid forty-five minute fielding drills?' he exploded. 'What I need is to bowl a few balls in the nets and then sit in the dressing room, have a smoke, a cuppa tea and think about the guys I have to bowl at today.'

'You should have played in our day,' I replied.

'I'd have loved to play with you guys,' he chuckled.

He would have been perfect for our era.

Maybe; maybe not. There is a pleasing kind of symmetry between the cricket values that Chappell espoused and those that Warne embraced – the absorption in the task, the commitment to the whole, the willingness to court defeat in the pursuit of victory. Yet they were not *quite* a perfect match. The Chappell family was steeped in the game on both sides. They treated cricket as a kind of Darwinian struggle, as a school of black-and-white thought. Cricketers in their semi-amateur era had need of such single-mindedness and self-discipline. There were no handouts, no guarantees, and precious little support: at the end of Chappell's thirty Tests as captain, he was only thirty-one, but exhausted, fed up and ready to hand the job over. Warne – well, of course, cricket *found him,* as he mooched by. He became a dedicated cricketer, but he was not by nature a dedicated man. He might well have fitted into the Australian dressing room of the 1970s, but it is hard to see how he would have made it there in the first place.

Whatever the case, the Australian coach appointed in November 1999 was not one of whom either Warne or Chappell were bound to approve. Donnish 46-year-old Queenslander John Buchanan had obtained his first coaching qualification as a means of making pocket money as a teenager at Brisbane's Greg Chappell Cricket Centre. He took it up more seriously after completing a degree in Human Movement at the University of Queensland, then more seriously still when his seven-match career as a Sheffield Shield opening batsman petered out. His earnest, painstaking and sometimes lateral methods were vindicated by Queensland's inaugural Shield victory after sixty-eight years of striving, and he soon made a snug fit in the Australian set-up with Steve Waugh.

I was a big wrap for 'Buck', having watched him mould the Queensland side into the best Shield team in the 1990s and been especially impressed by the way he had helped to change their culture by working away diligently in the background. I saw him more as a 'performance manager' than a coach, in that he would address a variety of issues, many not necessarily cricket related, and would endeavour to have each player prepared for his cricket with a clear mind so that the actual playing side would be easier. With Buck and me on a similar wavelength, both of us wanting to provoke, stimulate and challenge the members of the team to be the best they could possibly be, we set about putting a healthy work environment and a strong framework in place.

Buchanan, in turn, intuited that his most important relationship was with Waugh, beneath whose outward circumspection lurked a yearning to experiment and explore. By the end of his career, Waugh would be as well known for exchanging pleasantries with Mother Teresa and Nelson Mandela as for exchanging unpleasantries with Curtly Ambrose. Buchanan offered him that licence, and in a sense pardoned any excesses: when copies of *Tuesdays with Morrie* and *Who Moved My Cheese?* were distributed, they could be dismissed as a wheeze of the coach's.

Warne and Buchanan were never destined to be on the same page; they were hardly in the same book. At Buchanan's introductory team meeting, he said that he aimed to improve his charges as 'people first and cricketers second', and to stimulate their minds. Warne was perplexed. Was this the coach's job? What if he liked himself the way he was? What if his mind didn't need stimulating? And who was Buchanan anyway? Some guy who'd gotten lucky, who'd coached a red-hot Queensland team that had been going to win the Shield anyway. Bob Simpson and Geoff Marsh: at least they had gone out and done the business for Australia. Buchanan?

He looked like he'd be an easy wicket in the backyard.

Warne said the right things, in public at least, and in Buchanan's first eighteen months as coach had little to quibble with: Australia sustained a pitch of excellence unexampled since the immediate aftermath of World War II, losing only six of 35 one-day internationals and winning sixteen consecutive Tests. Differences between the pair finally surfaced when that streak was broken at Eden Gardens by India, who surged from behind to win an epic Test in March 2001. Barely recovered from a broken finger and far from match-fit, Warne palpably struggled, and Buchanan dared say so: 'Warnie's quite distressed when he comes off the field all the time. It's no secret that he's not one of the fittest characters running around in world cricket.' Asked if Warne's place was safe for the final Test at Chepauk, Buchanan was noncommittal and unenthused: 'I'm not saying he's going to be left out, he's still in the frame, but when we walk into this [next] Test, we've really got to have eleven blokes who can give five days of hard cricket and not be affected by any physical limitations.'

'In the frame'? Three hundred and seventy-four Test wickets and he was 'in the frame'? The media were apt to pass smartarse commentary on his fitness, Warne thought, but this was *his coach* – a coach, moreover, who had never stepped on a Test-match field, let alone one in India. A long *froideur* followed that in some respects was never really repaired, because Warne's irritation chimed so readily with Chappell's conviction that national coaches were – and if it was said once, it was said a million times – for driving you to and from the ground.

That Buchanan and Waugh formed such a tight unit gave the

debate a personal edge, Warne's dissidence where Buchanan was concerned becoming a kind of low-level critique of Waugh's captaincy. 'People such as Shane have not spent the time, prior to criticizing me, to learn what I do, why I do it, and what my motives and reasons are,' Buchanan grumbled. 'Such criticisms are not based on any well-thought-out position. Frankly, they are simply emotional statements.' But Warne had always played on emotion, and he wasn't about to change for Buchanan.

Chappell, meanwhile, assailed Buchanan mercilessly: 'If I had a son, the last person I'd send him to for coaching would be John Buchanan.' And the more time went on, the more he opined that Waugh's whole captaincy tenure had been a mistake, a lost opportunity:

If the selectors . . . had been really brave they would have given Warne the captaincy following Mark Taylor's successful reign. He would have been the right age and at his peak as a bowler. He would not only have made the cricket interesting for his players but also exciting for the crowds. None of this 'let's grind the opposition into the turf' for Warne.

Waugh quietly chafed at Chappell's baleful influence, feeling that he 'sweated on my blunders' and always reported them with a 'told you so' mentality, and wondering also at his sway over Warne.

In the clash of personalities, there *was* a kind of lost opportunity, for there *were* questions worth asking about the influence, and even the necessity, of national coaches. The problem with the argument against them was that it pretended the world had not changed, which it had. The first-class game had dwindled, other formats had multiplied, and there were resources available where there had not been before. With the advent of the AIS Cricket Academy, furthermore, young players were increasingly developed and groomed in a coach-intensive environment, and a national coach was a natural outgrowth of that culture. It's easy to apply the 'drover's dog' tag to Buchanan's career, as Bill Hayden pre-emptively designated Bob Hawke's prime ministership. The fact is that some team members felt better for his presence, and to the agnostics he did little harm.

Yet the argument against national coaches also had force, because of the tendency over time of bureaucracy to make work for itself, and to foster a culture of dependence that justifies its existence. Bob Simpson may or may not have been sincere when he described his objective as being to render himself redundant, but it was a worthwhile one. Especially after Waugh retired, Buchanan looked like someone trying to find a purpose for his position rather than knowing it instinctively; he indulged in activity for activity's sake, making pilgrimages to Alex Ferguson and Edward de Bono, dressing up commonplace ideas in jargon about 'unlocking the compartments', 'releasing the handbrakes' and 'avoiding the noise invasion'. When called upon to exert genuine knowhow in England in 2005, Buchanan had little to offer but clouds of abstraction. Even Adam Gilchrist felt his heart harden towards a coach he had always valued: 'When he came up with one of his left-field suggestions, guys were ignoring him now. The notion of us being "challenged" by his innovations had worn thin.'

Never dependent on such challenges, Warne was impervious to their diminished effectiveness, and kept his scepticism low-key.

'I am not sure we did a lot wrong . . . but I would say that behind the scenes we had a lot of team meetings which I'm not sure were always very productive,' he ventured coolly after the Ashes of 2005. 'I'm not saying that's the reason but it was just talking around in circles rather than getting out and doing something.' He made his point a little more directly in *My Illustrated Career* the following year, in which Buchanan's only appearance is in a photograph of him wielding a camcorder for no apparent reason while bearing an uncanny resemblance to Jerry Lewis in *The Nutty Professor.* 'Perhaps he's had an idea for the next team meeting,' reads Warne's droll caption.

When Buchanan in August 2006 ran his celebrated 'boot camp', Warne openly regarded it as risible. How would the team be improved by a cross between a male bonding retreat and a corporate off-site? He made his most explicit, Chappell-channelling comments yet: 'International players know how to play. You don't need a coach getting too technical. You can forget that you just need to bowl the ball.' When he arrived, Warne presented five packets of cigarettes as his 'dependent medication'. Buchanan was intrigued when Warne later told him he had learned 'three things' from the camp, and asked what they were. 'I'm fat, I'm a weak prick, and I want to go home,' answered Warne.

The strain of putting up with each other all those years manifests itself in little ways even now. Buchanan's instructional book, *Learning from Legends,* grants only the most cursory reference to the greatest legend of all. Warne's ranking of his hundred greatest players, *Shane Warne's Century*, lists Waugh, whom at one stage he regarded as a better batsman than either Sachin Tendulkar or

Brian Lara, at number 26, and praises him with a succession of faint damns: 'He was a good all-round player, and he knew his game . . . I am pretty aggressive about the way I play the game; Waugh took a more conservative approach and he wasn't a big risk-taker . . . He really was a good player, and like other good batsmen he improved as he went on.' For his part, Waugh finally got off his chest a few encoded irritations about Warne in his *Out of My Comfort Zone*, albeit he secreted them carefully in its bulk.

Tottenham Hotspurs' famed striker Steve Archibald famously made the observation that team spirit was an illusion glimpsed in the aftermath of victory. To apply it to Australia in its halcyon recent era would be unduly cynical; by the same token, the frequency of victory did much to alleviate those tensions and variances that did arise. Common purpose is far easier to come by when it is so availing so frequently.

FOUR

THE TRIALS OF WARNE

'GOOD TO SEE YOU, Shane,' said Herschelle Gibbs when he bumped into his old nemesis at the Indian Premier League in 2010. 'It's always good to be seen, Hersch,' Warne replied.

Well, perhaps not exactly *always*. There were surely times as controversy roiled around him when Warne must have longed for a cloak of invisibility or a new identity to relieve him of *being* Shane Warne. But maybe not so frequently as others might have. That he wandered into mishap and misadventure as often as he did sometimes suggested an unconscious relish for it – a curiosity about what would happen if he pressed this button, pressed this point, pressed this flesh. At times he used to remind me of the scene in the comedy *Peep Show* where the incorrigible Jez realises he is about to sleep with his flatmate Mark's girlfriend. 'This is almost certainly the wrong thing to do,' he reflects. 'But if I don't do it, how will I know?'

Warne fast became Australia's number-one cricketer. He also, just as quickly, became its only genuine cricket 'personality'. This was confusing. We are commonly taught to distinguish between true fame, rich and nourishing, based on genuine accomplishment, and junk fame, the too-sweet, too-salty, empty calories of celebrity, a paltry and perishable substitute. Warne radiated both, creating two broad and parallel streams of news, one based on what he had done, usually on the cricket field, and the other derived from who he was, usually off it. There were exceptions, and intersections, but in general Warne lived both existences to the full, as a star sportsman, and sporting star. He did what came naturally – sometimes, as became known, to a fault. 'Leg spin bowlers get into trouble if they have second thoughts,' he once said. In daily life, though, second thoughts can be prudent.

The chronicle of Warne sensations is a long, if not an interminable one. A majority stem from what we are sometimes apt to call 'private life', except that in Warne's case this formulation makes little sense, his life having been relentlessly public, with a strange kind of general collusion. Where most celebrities are concerned, there is usually at least an affectation of distaste about violations of privacy. I never read a word along these lines where Warne was concerned. Warne's privacy was serially invaded, his dirty laundry flown from flagpoles, the justification being that he was a public figure and therefore . . . well, fair game. He was out there. He was up for it. So he had it coming to him, didn't he? And wasn't he, on occasion, bad? Warne's protests that his indiscretions, especially his extramarital misadventures, were not really anyone's business but his own, were airily dismissed. Well, to invoke Mandy Rice-Davies, he would say that, wouldn't he?

In a sense, of course, he was fair game – or, at least, fairer game than most. He was a young white male athlete, pampered and privileged, lauded and lionised. Often enough, too, he *had* done the wrong thing, mainly by his long-suffering wife. All the same, by late standards of the behaviour of prominent athletes, Warne does not come off too badly. He has never broken the law. He has no recorded history of violence. He has never gambled to excess, and now prefers the protected environs of high-end poker. He has never wrestled with alcohol or been addicted to a drug, unless you count the TaiSlim Shakes that helped him achieve his newly sylph-like shape. His other weaknesses have been open, acknowledged and utterly prosaic: in full public view, he has worked to reverse his hair loss, battled with his weight, and striven to stop smoking. That he found himself 'in trouble' such a staggering proportion of the time, then, tells us both something about Warne and something about his media chorus.

It was not unprecedented for Shane Warne to achieve fame and recognition as young as he did, even in a game as purportedly staid as cricket. 'He was news,' wrote C.L.R. James of W.G. Grace, 'and as he continually broke all precedents before he had passed his middle twenties, each amazing new performance told the public, cricketing and otherwise, that here was one of those rare phenomena, something that had never been seen before and was not likely to be seen again.' Bradman published his autobiography aged twenty-two, and within a few years was probably the best known commoner in the Empire. But when 23-year-old Warne bowled the Ball of the Century, he was making his mark on a new world with new rules, new codes and new expectations.

Warne's lifetime spans the rise and rise of sport as a commercial property. When Warne was growing up in Melbourne in the 1970s, sport was straightforwardly compartmentalised and simply seasonal. There was football on Saturday afternoons in winter, experienced primarily by radio; in the evening, a quarter or two of the match of the day might be replayed on Channel Seven. Through summer, cricket was on ABC radio and also on ABC television, shot from one end, and without advertisements. Television featured one omnibus sports programme: Seven's *World of Sport* on Sunday afternoons. The sport sections of the newspapers, meanwhile, were comparatively small and unambitious, Australians consuming their sport soberly, and sports writers meeting that market.

That apparatus made a good match for a society into which even the most successful sporting practitioners blended inconspicuously. Bradman represented something like the gold standard of Australian sporting fame: few figures as equivalently accomplished in a popular pursuit can have lived, and been permitted to live, so close to an ordinary life. The Don held ordinary jobs, as a seller of sporting goods and a dealer in stocks, and raised an ordinary family with his childhood sweetheart in the only house he ever owned. Nobody who wished to could not find Bradman's address, and all who wrote to 2 Holden Street, Kensington Park were guaranteed a response. But out of this developed a stable, sustainable, long-term, arm's-length relationship between Bradman and his public, in which both, consciously and unconsciously, honoured their sides of the bargain. Thus did a pre-modern fame endure into a post-modern age, a compromise classically of Australia – a country exalting the common man.

It was cricket, nonetheless, that then led the charge out of the short-back-and-sides era. Kerry Packer's breakaway troupe, World Series Cricket, accentuated panache as much as prowess. The Chappells, Lillee, Marsh, Hookes, Walters, Walker: these were characters, bristling, swaggering and instantly recognisable. Before the inaugural Supertest, the Australian players were actually lectured by their countryman John Newcombe, who had become part of a makeover of American tennis by joining agent Dave Dixon's 'Handsome Eight' ten years earlier: this octet of ruggedly good-looking male players formed the inner core of the World Championship Tennis circuit that helped usher in the open age. 'When I started to have a court personality like the one I had in private, more people turned up to watch me play,' Newcombe explained. 'Image is important, no matter what the traditionalists say and how much they hate it.'

It was advice taken to heart by both the players and their promoters, and this new sway of star power, the value embedded in the charisma of a sport's top talent, drew a fascinated audience. It presaged the emergence in the 1980s of a new kind of Australian sports hero, known as much by their images as by their accomplishments: Pat Cash, Greg Norman, Jan Stephenson, Rob de Castella, Jeff Fenech, Warwick Capper, Grant Kenny, Peter Brock, Raelene Boyle, the Mean Machine, the Oarsome Foursome. Warne's favourite footballer, Hawthorn's Dermott Brereton, was identified as much by his dyed-blond perm as by his body-clashing aggression. Television ceased merely to be sport's silent witness; it became its narrator, exchequer and unacknowledged legislator.

Television was always bound to love Warne. His gifts were sublimely telegenic. In showing Warne off, television showed its own potential for bringing the viewer closer to the action, offering over and again the opportunity to ask: Did that ball just do what I think it did? Consider Jonathan Agnew's call of Warne's Ball of the Century: 'Shane Warne, off only two or three paces. He bowls and Gatting is taken on the pad. He's bowled? [pause] Well, Gatting's still standing there, he can't believe it. That must have turned a very long way, we haven't got a view of this, we'll have to wait for a replay to tell you exactly what happened.' You had to see Bradman to believe him; you had to see Warne *again* to believe him. And no matter how many times you watched Warne, say, bowling Shivnarine Chanderpaul in Sydney in November 1996, the ball bouncing out of the rough like a zombie rising from the grave, it never palled. Fifteen years later, it enjoys a rich afterlife on YouTube, something not even invented at the time.

In the early part of his career, Warne enveloped his prestidigitation in a further layer of intrigue by talking about this or that 'mystery ball' he was working on with Jenner. One of his earliest promotions, for Nike, was based around a delivery that capered round Australia before dismissing Ian Botham. 'In reality, there was never any new ball,' admitted Bob Simpson, and Warne soon seemed to realise that the novelty of such threats would wear off. He developed instead an almost Assangesque attitude to secrecy, confident always that it was one thing to be told about a delivery, quite another to play it – revealing in doing so the expository skills that Warne has more recently applied to commentary. The novelist Tony Wilson has described watching Warne give one of his televised tutorials on leg spin, concluding it with the throwaway line, 'I've got my plan, and then I just have to execute it.' As Wilson observes, Warne wannabes everywhere 'must laugh at the casual way he throws out those five little words: "just have to execute it"'.

Warne the showman, moreover, had what they call in the advertising game 'cut-through'. His cricket was brand-new while also connecting with ancient lore, palpably aggressive while also being endlessly subtle. And while the football codes have come to hog a handsome share of sport's bandwidth in the past two decades, there are hundreds of footballers; Warne only ever had ten other cricketers in the national team to share the limelight with, none matching him for flash and flair. What Spurs' Danny Blanchflower said of his own game counts little less for cricket: 'The great fallacy is that the game is first and last about winning. It's nothing of the kind. It's about glory. It's about doing things in style, with a flourish, about going out and beating the other lot, not waiting for them to die of boredom.' The cricketers led to world supremacy by Mark Taylor, Steve Waugh and Ricky Ponting were relentless, superbly drilled, devastatingly efficient, but it was Warne who imparted their sheen of glory.

And the life? It was as true as it was tautological, Warne was Warne: sunny, suggestible, boyish, bumptious, reckless, feckless. Ramachandra Guha once observed that Sachin Tendulkar had been constructed by his country's fourth estate as 'the only flawless Indian'; Warne was not quite constructed in this country as 'the only flawed Australian', but there was deemed to be something uniquely outsize about his appetites and his aberrations.

In his early days, Warne appropriated for his own use the popular tagline of the Melbourne broadcaster and controversialist Derryn Hinch: 'Expect the unexpected.' It wasn't a bad motto for a leg spinner, but Warne was arguably better suited to Hinch's public persona as 'the Human Headline'. In the rest of this chapter, I want to look at the stories behind three of those headlines, their circumstances, and their consequences.

Newspaper stories don't start the day before headlines go to press. There is always a context, always a set of preconditions. In revisiting Warne's brush with match-fixing, you must wind back the clock another six months or so to an apparently unrelated incident that exerted a subtle influence on ensuing events.

In March 1994, Warne played in Australia's first Test in South Africa since 1970, an excellent match played in a sulphurous atmosphere. Here was an exception to the rule that modern cricketers barely get to know the countries they visit. Weeks before the country's first post-apartheid election, South Africa was a country on edge, in denial about its past while profoundly uncertain about its future, but determined to celebrate its return to the circle of Test nations. Attention on the Australians was acute, incessant and sometimes overpowering. Ian Healy jestingly dubbed Warne 'Elvis' in honour of his conspicuousness; he was a 24-year-old who needed chaperoning by armed bodyguards. For the first time, perhaps, Warne began feeling ambivalently about his fame, and hankering for a moment's anonymity. 'I feel as if I'm burning up inside,' he told an interviewer.

Then he did. To walk onto the field, the players had to negotiate a forty-metre race thronged by jeering South African spectators, who grew ever more triumphal as their team edged ahead. For the first forty-three overs of South Africa's second innings, Warne undertook various boundary fielding assignments that exposed him to the brunt of the crowd's abuse. When he bowled opening batsman Andrew Hudson round his legs with his first ball, Warne unleashed a proportional tirade, baying at the retreating batsman like a one-man mob; umpire David Shepherd called it, euphemistically, 'the soldier's farewell'. Merv Hughes, who had taken a similar pizzling from spectators, had earlier done likewise on dismissing Hudson's partner Gary Kirsten.

Warne afterwards was genuinely mortified, particularly as soft-spoken, God-fearing Hudson was actually a well-liked opponent. Although he was not actually reported by the umpires, Shepherd and local Barry Lambson, Warne was not surprised when he and also Hughes were summoned to face the International Cricket Council match referee, Englishman Donald Carr. 'Reckon this is it,' he told Hudson's teammate Allan Donald. 'They'll suspend me for sure.' In fact, Carr stayed his hand. The ICC code of conduct was not two years old, and had not previously been used to penalise a player for a 'send-off'. Carr seems to have been loath to apply it speculatively under circumstances where duress may have been involved, and fined the two Victorians a token amount (1000 rand, about $400).

Back in Australia, very few people saw the episodes live, but more and more saw the replays, which, divorced from their context, were damning. For some time, the Australian Cricket Board chairman Alan Crompton and chief executive Graham Halbish had been talking tough about player misbehaviour; from afar, at least, these offences seemed to fit that bill perfectly. On the last day, Hughes also remonstrated fiercely with a spectator needling him as he walked off the ground after being dismissed, sharpening the image of the Australians as boors and buffoons; opinion makers lined up to argue that their administrators would be delinquent if they failed to take their own action. So it was that the day after the Test ended in defeat for Australia, the Australian Cricket Board fined Warne and Hughes $4000 each for providing 'a totally inappropriate role model for young Australians to follow' – to that time the heaviest such fines ever levied.

The objective may have been laudable, but the execution was crude and the result sour. Natural justice was poorly served. The two cricketers had already been disciplined by an international body under a code to which Australia was a party; the Board had then come along and disciplined them again, punitively, from 10 000 miles away, without talking to them, their captain, their coach or their team manager, without hearing a plea in mitigation, without provision for appeal. Australia would later lecture other countries about usurping ICC disciplinary procedures while conveniently forgetting that it had been the first country to do so.

News of the fines broke over the Australians like a thunderclap – they had been abused, they had been defeated, and now, as Steve Waugh put it, they had been belittled 'for the sake of the Board wanting the public's sympathy'. Visiting board officials were requested to avoid the Australian dressing room for the rest of the tour, and bad blood lingered. Ian Healy thought that the ensuing year was the 'lowest ebb' in the players' relationship with their administrators, which stiffened their resolve, among other things, to form a collective body to represent them: 'It was near impossible to form a bond with men we never saw and didn't know, who had great power in Australian cricket, made important decisions about Australian cricket, but rarely seemed accountable for those decisions.'

This background is useful, because it is usually left out of a subsequent, far graver saga, when players and administrators lacked the cohesion and trust to cope with the bane of match-fixing. It is also worth going into subsequent events in some detail, given the fancy and fantasy that has flourished around them. In hindsight, we were all naïve – rubes, pushovers, easy marks.

To those in the Anglosphere, gambling on cricket had until the early 1990s perfectly normal, healthy and sociable associations. Even after the celebrated bet by Dennis Lillee and Rod Marsh on England at 500–1 at Headingley in 1981, there remained no taboo about players betting on themselves and others. Before the 1993 Ashes series, for example, Steve Waugh put £25 on himself at 8–1 in an English betting tent to top the Australian aggregates – not in secret either, for he described it in his first *Ashes Diary*, and nobody batted an eyelid. There was only a dim awareness of the vigorous subterranean market on the subcontinent in illegally offering odds on international cricket. It existed in the corners of the cricket map captioned 'Here be monsters'.

The Australians approached their 1994 tour of the subcontinent with other apprehensions in mind. Things had a way of going pentangle-shaped in Pakistan. Doctored pitches, restive crowds, tendentious umpires, hard-to-get alcohol: for Australians, this was a hardship posting. Six years earlier, a team led by Allan Border had almost walked out of a tour, so incandescent was their rage about the standard of the officiation. Their coach on this trip, Simpson, was the same; so was their manager, Col Egar, a classic Australian cricketing gerontocrat who ran the South Australian Cricket Association like a personal fiefdom, and who liked managing teams in the subcontinent because deferential locals mistook his Christian name for an abbreviation of 'Colonel'. The retirement of Allan Border had brought forth a thoughtful leader in Mark Taylor, but this would be a trip requiring some tact, sensitivity and responsibility – not qualities easily willed into existence if they do not arise naturally.

Before the tour, the Board cautiously retained a Sydney public-relations firm to provide players with pat answers to stock questions: 'Harsh conditions are part of international cricket,' 'Weather conditions during a hot Australian summer are just as challenging for touring teams,' and 'Conditions in Pakistan are very comfortable: five-star accommodation, hotel-prepared food at the grounds and bottled water.' Thanks for asking; have a nice day.

There were first some Sri Lankan preliminaries: the Singer World Series, a one-day tournament dogged by poor weather and lack-lustre performances. Australia's opening game seemed to be played in slow motion, Pakistan limping to nine for 151 in 50 overs to lose to Australia by 28 runs. 'Why are these guys blocking everything?' Steve Waugh asked himself during his spell. 'Am I really bowling that well that they can't get me off the square on such a flat, batsman-friendly pitch?' At the time, however, such questions tended to be set aside: such was Pakistan, a cricket riddle inside a conundrum wrapped in an enigma. Warne, who clouted an unbeaten 30 before taking three for 29, was not complaining.

Between times, there were opportunities for recreation of a kind that would shortly be off limits, the gambling exploits of Mark Waugh and Shane Warne at a casino neighbouring the Oberoi Hotel becoming the subject of some merriment in the Australian camp. One night, Mark Waugh tossed a chip onto a roulette table and told the croupier lightly, 'Wherever it lands, mate.' Healy recalled: 'It landed on number 20, which, of course, immediately came up. Only Junior could have done that, or so it seemed as he calmly collected his chips and strolled, with no fuss, towards the cashier's window.' Warne was less lucky, losing heavily.

It was at the casino that Mark Waugh met a figure whom he could only later recall as 'John': investigators concluded that 'John' was an alias of Mukesh Kumar Gupta, a former Delhi bank clerk turned bookmaker who had already cultivated links with several Indian players, including Ajay Sharma and Manoj Prabhakar. They struck a 'business deal': Waugh accepted $US4000 from 'John' in return for pre-match intelligence in forthcoming games, specifically concerning pitch and weather conditions. On request, Waugh introduced his new friend to Warne as 'John, who bets on the cricket'. Having been invited to John's room and accepted various blandishments, Warne also accepted an envelope bulging with $US5000 in cash: 'I asked what it was for and he said it was a token of his appreciation and compensation for the money I had lost the evening before . . . He was quite persistent and said that he would be offended if I didn't take it.' Warne later lost this money too.

Why did Waugh and Warne acquiesce in these offers? Did it not confuse them that they were being offered so much money for so apparently little? Did it not strike them as just a little bit odd that an Asian gentleman was calling himself John? On Australia's previous visit to Sri Lanka, it transpired, both Dean Jones and Greg Matthews had been approached by, and had rebuffed, cash-wielding strangers. On this trip, senior members of the party were leery of too-friendly strangers, and some quiet warnings were issued.

But top sportsmen are regularly in receipt of monies based on who they are rather than what they might do. What, after all, are endorsement contracts and sponsorship deals? People want to know them, people want to help them; that some people would also wish to slip them a few bucks would seem on face value to fit on that continuum. Or at least, it did in Sri Lanka at that time. Here were Warne and Waugh, stuck in a country neither of them knew anything about, playing a tournament nobody would remember. The scenario had only one beguiling quality: it was *away*; away from home, away from attention, away from responsibility. Remember that timeworn commandment of Australian sport: 'What happens on tour stays on tour.' Remember Mencken: 'Conscience is the inner voice that warns us somebody may be looking.' Frankly, in Sri Lanka in 1994, conscience could take the day off.

In Mark Waugh's case, his familiarity with punting, and fondness for harness-racing in particular, was well known. He had just struck a sponsorship deal to promote the Miracle Mile, and acquired a share in a breeding syndicate. He liked a win, and 'John' was offering him a piece of the action in which he could not lose. I suspect that, for all his easygoing nature, Waugh was more covetous of money than he let on, possibly because his shrewd and industrious brother Steve was so adept at accumulating it. Mark remains the only Australian cricketer who has ever asked me for money for an interview, a year before his casino encounter. When I explained that I could not afford to pay him – and I remember this vividly – he grumbled as if partly to himself: 'Seems like the things I do never lead to money.' Perhaps he thought it was time that changed.

In Warne's case, 'John' came with the prior approval of Waugh – and that counted for a lot. Waugh was cool. Waugh was lucky. Warne thought they were alike – laid-back, fond of a flutter, up for a lark. Like his sometime media patron Kerry Packer, Warne was also partial to cash, inveterately sporting a wallet that bulged with notes. Now, aged twenty-four, he was being offered an envelope of readies by an admirer introduced to him by a trusted teammate, in an anonymous hotel room, in a faraway country, with no strings attached and no questions asked – *just for being himself.* He would not have anticipated that a report of this act in the *Sydney Morning Herald* some four years hence would be headlined 'Baggy

Green Shame' – because, frankly, nobody could have.

Which is not to say that alert antennae would not at the time have detected some disturbing signals – several other games in the tournament were cited in subsequent corruption investigations. Rumours were circulating by the time the Australians embarked from Colombo for Karachi, including one that Pakistan had deliberately dawdled to defeat against Australia, and might even themselves have put money on their opponents. Manager Egar asked Pakistan's coach Intikhab Alam, for whom he was carrying duty-free alcohol through customs; Intikhab denied it.

In fact, Intikhab would later testify to the judicial inquiry into match-fixing chaired by Justice Malik Mohammad Qayyum that on the night of the Pakistan v Australia match he had accepted a 'furious' call from an anonymous complainant claiming to have lost a large sum of money on the game because four or five players had been 'bought'. Intikhab also testified that his former team-mate Asif Iqbal had shared with him a startling confidence: 'He told me bluntly that bookies had lost Rs 40 lac and they wanted to recover same at any cost. I had known Asif Iqbal since very long and was shocked to hear what he said to me.' But the corruption of cricket had already been accommodated by a climate of denial and evasion.

On arrival in Karachi, Egar then attended a private dinner at which guests busily placed phone bets with local bookmakers on games and even points in a women's tennis match they were watching on television. 'This business in Sri Lanka,' he said cautiously to his host. 'I'm led to believe your blokes backed Australia.' The reply took him aback: 'I wouldn't be surprised. I can tell you that the [local] bookmakers are connected to the bookmakers in Bombay and the Emirates. They've got $US2.5 million to buy the Pakistan team.' When Egar scoffed, the host looked serious: 'No, really. $US2.5 million. And I'm led to believe that half of them have been bought already.' Again, however, Egar issued no warning to and made no inquiries of his players.

The First Test was played at Karachi's National Stadium, a stark concrete bowl laid with hallowed Pakistani turf where the hosts had never lost a Test. The Australians, nonetheless, finished the fourth day buoyant: Pakistan needed 158 to win from its last seven wickets on a dusty, wearing pitch. Just before the close, Australia had taken the vital wicket of Pakistan's captain Salim Malik, so he could now be removed from calculations. Or could he?

At about 10.30 pm, the telephone rang in the Pearl Continental Hotel suite that Warne was sharing with his fellow slow bowler Tim May. When Warne answered, it was Malik. An exorbitantly gifted player of slow bowling, Malik had come to Pakistan's captaincy by default because of irreconcilable differences between the two other candidates, Wasim Akram and Waqar Younis. He gave off, nonetheless, a faintly seedy odour. His colleagues at Essex County Cricket Club referred to him ironically as 'Honest Sal', and remembered him for asking, after receiving his first pay slip: 'Tax? What is tax?' The Australians, for their part, called him 'the Rat', because of his murine features, and if ever a man could be said to have grown into his nickname, it was Malik.

Without giving an explanation, Malik now serenely invited Warne and May to his suite. May groaned that he was too tired, but Warne was perhaps a little intrigued, having never really spoken to

Malik, while respecting his batsmanship. History might have taken a different course had May not preferred to loll about on his bed that evening. As it was, Warne ventured forth on his own, walking into an encounter for which nothing in his background could have quite prepared him.

We chatted briefly about the first four days and then he said: 'You know, we cannot lose.' My immediate reaction was that he just wanted to sound confident. I laughed and suggested that we felt we were in with a good chance. He repeated it once, before saying: 'You don't understand, we cannot lose.' When I asked what he meant he finally came out with his offer – $200,000 cash to be made available in half an hour for Tim May and myself to bowl badly the following day. 'Both of you bowl outside off stump and it will be a draw,' he said.

Exactly how the conversation ended has never quite been clear – in the various accounts, the action more or less dissolves from Malik making the offer to Warne returning to his room. What happened and how Warne felt in that intervening period I doubt we shall ever know. First, one suspects, there would have been confusion. Was the offer a joke? A ruse? A snare? Genuine? It could not, surely, be genuine. Two hundred thousand dollars to bowl badly? Two hundred thousand dollars to draw a Test? Could it really be worth that much? In cash? Two hundred thousand dollars was more money than Warne would earn from cricket that whole year: it must, at least momentarily, have boggled his mind.

But then, how did this whole idea compute? In their numerous self-absolutions afterwards, Australian cricketers have referred to match-fixing as an Australian taboo: Aussies *always* play to win. Yet there is nothing peculiarly Australian about this. Fundamental to any game, observed the sociologist Anatol Rapoport, is the 'assumption of similarity' – the idea that 'one's opponent intends to win if he can', and that, in attempting this, he will be influenced by 'similar considerations' and the 'same kinds of strategies'. To find an opponent who was not in this respect a mirror image would have disoriented Warne the man, not Warne the Australian.

One other aspect of the conversation between Warne and Malik deserves remark, at least as Warne tells it. Gambling goes unmentioned. Malik insists simply that his team 'cannot lose'. He does not explain it in terms of needing to do so for bookmaking interests; he does not say that he is acting as an agent for the $200 000; he says, apparently, nothing more than that money would be forthcoming in the event of the Australians' agreement. In retrospect, it seems highly probable that Malik was acting for Gupta, Gupta's original approaches to Warne and Waugh in Sri Lanka having been to soften them up and sound them out; that they would be Malik's targets in Pakistan is simply too much of a coincidence. But at this time the connection was not so obvious.

Today, the idea that bookmakers stake money on particular results is integral to our understanding of cricket corruption, and to our construction of it as the most heinous of crimes against the game; in 1994, Malik might simply have appeared to be protecting himself, his captaincy and Pakistan's proud record in Karachi, and the money might have been his, or the Pakistan Cricket Board's, or that of various anonymous malefactors.

'What did the Rat want?' May asked when Warne walked back into their room, and was initially incredulous when told. 'I bowl outside off stump anyway,' he joked. 'I'd be taking money for nothing.' Gradually, the Australians' attitude hardened: May urged Warne to ring Malik back with a defiant promise that Australia would 'nail them' the next day. In fact, the game came down to the wire, the hosts preserving their Karachi ascendancy with a 54-run last-wicket stand. It was a devastating captaincy debut for Taylor, who had made a pair, lost a game that must almost have seemed unlosable, and was then required to front the match referee with a junior pace bowler who had been censured for appealing too extravagantly. Warne picked an unfortunate moment in the aftermath in the dressing room to confide laconically: 'By the way, Tubs. We got offered money to bowl badly today by Salim Malik.' Taylor groaned inwardly: 'I didn't need to hear that.' So, for the time being, he acted as though he had not.

This was a debacle in the making, as much cultural as procedural. A gulf separated the Australians and the Pakistanis, of course. But the cultures within the Australian camp also barely overlapped: a generation of young men who wanted to win games of cricket and have a good time doing so, and a group of considerably older men who wanted them to win but within the bounds of propriety. Neither group was quite comfortable round the other. All they could just about agree on was that nobody wanted a repeat of Pakistan in '88, or of Johannesburg in '94. Malcolm Knox has found particular fault with the captain: 'It's easy to imagine Border, or Steve Waugh, marching to Malik's room and having it out face-to-face.' But it's not entirely clear what this would have accomplished, except inciting Malik to frenzied denials, plunging the series into crisis. And the touring party was under orders that that should not happen. Everyone repeat after me: 'Harsh conditions are part of international cricket', 'Conditions in Pakistan are very comfortable', etc.

They weren't, of course, and they were growing less comfortable by the day. It wasn't only players and administrators who were out of their depth in an environment in which corruption was so pervasive: when Australia met South Africa in the Wills Triangular Series at Faisalabad, for example, journalists were astonished to find their newly connected phones ringing within minutes with calls from bookmakers in Bombay. And because no action had been taken, the jeopardy remained. When Australia arrived in Rawalpindi the day after and attended a crowded and noisy reception, it was Mark Waugh's turn to be accosted by Malik: 'I'll offer you $US200 000. I'll have it in your hotel tonight if you get four or five players and you throw the game tomorrow.' When they were swiftly separated by the social swirl, Waugh sought out Warne, who suggested they consult Steve.

'Tell him to fuck off,' Steve advised. Mark assented: 'About an hour and a half later I went up to him [Malik] and told him that we didn't play the game that way. That's it. End of story.'

It was barely the beginning.

The next day, Waugh made 121 from 134 balls out of five for 250, only for Australia to be smashed by nine wickets by the same team that six weeks earlier had taken eleven more overs to make a hundred runs fewer – that enigma of Pakistan cricket again. On returning to the dressing room, Waugh broke the stunned silence with a jest: 'Ah, we would have been better off taking the bribes, guys.'

Simpson's ears pricked. It was by now nearly three weeks since that fated night at the Pearl Continental, and word of Malik's approaches had finally reached someone interested in doing something about them. It was Simpson who would inform Col Egar and ICC chief executive David Richards; he also urged Egar to inform Crompton and Halbish. Of all the officials involved, Simpson, old enough and ugly enough to be unconcerned by diplomatic niceties, is probably the only one deserving of credit. But his standing had been affected by his involvement in the players' insurrection six years earlier, and his influence was waning: indispensable to Border, he was finding less of a role to play with Taylor. Among other administrators in the know, there grew an anxiety that if the allegations were aired, the Pakistan Cricket Board would cancel the balance of the tour. If everyone just held their nerve . . .

When Taylor's team returned home, there was, at least publicly, an air of self-congratulation. A Pakistan tour without visible incident: we did it! Everyone now settled in for a nice cosy Ashes series. The Australians kept their own counsel, and Waugh and Warne kept 'John's': Waugh later confessed to accepting ten phone calls, Warne to three. Both would stick to the story that no confidences were betrayed. Pitch and weather. Maybe a word about morale. Maybe a hint about selection. Innocuous stuff, the players have said – and it is quite credible. Waugh had convinced himself that he was telling 'John' no more than he told reporters and radio stations; Warne has always had a knack for saying nothing much at length. Gupta's contacts, furthermore, were more probably about staying connected to the players and keeping them on the hook than extracting information.

Crompton and Halbish at the ACB and Richards at the ICC, meanwhile, pushed matters quietly back and forth, making no further inquiries, not even alerting their counterparts in Pakistan. Remarkably, there is no evidence of any written report or briefing *by anyone* aware of the events until early February 1995, when highly specific inquiries from the veteran *Sydney Morning Herald* correspondent Phil Wilkins suggested that it might be a good idea to collect more detailed information: Warne, Waugh and May then all handwrote unsigned recollections of Malik's approaches. It's commonly assumed that Wilkins' informant was an agitated Simpson, impatient with lack of progress in the matter.

Wilkins' exclusive caused a predictable storm, immense bitterness in Pakistan, and a big problem in Australia – the problem was that, unbeknownst to the Australian Cricket Board, they knew only *part* of the story. Warne and Waugh had kept to themselves their continued contact with 'John', probably for two reasons: firstly, they had convinced themselves the communications were innocent, and that they were in control; secondly, they had little faith or trust in administrators who fined them for fleeting losses of temper and then, when confronted with truly dark misdeeds, found it all just a bit too difficult.

The other shoe was not to drop for a further two weeks, during New Zealand's one-day Centenary Series, which Australia won. Halbish asked the team's media manager, Ian McDonald, to investigate inquiries from Mark Ray of the *Sunday Age*, who had received an anonymous letter tipping him off that Warne and Waugh had received money from a bookmaker. The provenance of that letter has remained obscure – it might even have come from Gupta himself. Whatever the case, the pair came clean, perhaps because they did not believe there was a problem, perhaps because if there *was* a problem it now automatically became someone else's.

In fact, things would get worse for them before they got better. During the team's stopover in Sydney en route to the West Indies soon after, the pair were grilled at length by Crompton and Halbish, admitted to accepting money from 'John', and were heavily fined: Warne was docked $8000 and Waugh $10 000, roughly the extent of their misbegotten gains translated into Australian dollars. While many later faulted the penalties as paltry, they nonetheless broke the record set a year earlier in South Africa for disciplinary imposts on Australian cricketers.

Everyone knows what happened next: nothing. The fines were not actually revealed to the rest of the Board until the *end* of their meeting the next day, *after* the team had left for the Caribbean, and *after* directors had discussed the Malik affair with the ICC's David Richards, visiting from England. The directors were asked simply to ratify the penalties, and were hardly in a position to do otherwise; advised that there was no legal obligation to make those penalties public, they elected not to. Why? It was for 'the good of cricket'. Some thought it was already too late to do anything. Some believed that the revelations about 'John' would muddy the waters where the allegations against Malik were concerned. In one case, Egar's, there was almost certainly a belated sense of embarrassment: he had not even known about 'John', despite being on the spot.

At the back of each mind, too, there was the knowledge that

Australia was about to undertake an important tour, with a chance of bearding the West Indies in their own den for the first time in twenty years. Imagine at such a juncture having to suspend two such key players while an investigation took place – as Pakistan was about to do with Malik, when he returned from a tour of Zimbabwe and South Africa that had been streaked with further scandal. And if Australia were to recapture the Frank Worrell Trophy, *that* would be for the good of cricket. *Wouldn't it?*

This was something on which all could agree – the players too. In Ian Healy's words: 'I thought the Board's thinking was right – they wanted to protect the players – but, of course, I would think that.' Perhaps there was an incipient desire in both groups to achieve a rapprochement after a year of friction. Thus was struck a pact of silence that bound all involved for the next three and a half years, a pact that compromised efforts to properly investigate match-fixing, a pact that enabled Gupta to spread a web of influence that also ensnared South Africa's Hansie Cronje and India's Mohammad Azharuddin, and a pact that allowed Australia to secure its supremacy of international cricket without a speck against its name – for that series in the Caribbean was all that had been hoped for.

The irony is, of course, that Warne would later be repeatedly admonished during the controversies of his career for a tendency to shift blame and economise on the truth. Yet if he learned the want of candour anywhere, it might well have been from the Australian Cricket Board, who somehow convinced themselves that they could either veil their actions or ride out their eventual unveiling.

It's interesting to contemplate just what the various parties to that pact were able to do together over the years of their complicity. Not once in a board meeting in that time were the fines revisited. Simpson, Crompton and Halbish all lost their jobs for unrelated reasons, although Halbish then turned up on the other side of the barricades as an adviser to Warne, the Waughs and May at the newly formed Australian Cricketers' Association, while Egar remained part of a board that steadfastly opposed them. Warne wrote a cricket book with Ray as co-author without a sniff of 'John'; Taylor put his name to two cricket books that avoided even mentioning the Australians' allegations against Malik. Taylor and Mark Waugh returned to Pakistan on tour four years after events to testify at the hearings before Justice Qayyum in the Lahore High Court without volunteering any more detail than was already public.

But it was during an intermission in those proceedings that the tapestry woven tightly round events commenced unravelling, when a member of the PCB's legal team showed a letter to Malcolm Conn, a pertinacious journalist from *The Australian*, suggesting that Mark Waugh had been 'involved with a bookmaker' – it may have emanated from the same source as Ray's. Rather surprisingly, counsel for the PCB asked no questions along these lines, but Conn did, and he kept on asking until Halbish's successor Malcolm Speed conceded that not only had Waugh been involved but Warne too: the reporter had thrown out a sprat and caught a mackerel. In a sense, everything we now know of this chapter in Australian cricket hinges on two chance disclosures four years apart. What if Simpson had not been within earshot when Mark Waugh emitted his dressing-room quip? What if Conn not been nearby to receive his courtroom tip?

Most perverse was the effect of the four intervening years. During that hiatus, the reek around match-fixing had grown seedier. The Board's failure to perform anything other than the most perfunctory investigation appeared therefore more culpable, and the opprobrium suffered by Warne and Waugh was that much more intense – the very opposite of the objective of the initial cover-up. The two players were paraded at a press conference at the Adelaide Oval effectively in disgrace, read out statements during which they confessed to being 'naïve and stupid', then were ushered out of the room before any questions could be asked – ostensibly for their own protection, actually for the protection of the Australian Cricket Board. Looking like men with something to hide, Warne and Waugh incurred most of the popular ire, which did not always distinguish between their misdeeds and Malik's.

Still recovering from shoulder surgery, Warne was spared the ordeal of Mark Waugh during the ensuing Ashes Test, who was booed all the way to the wicket and off by a crowd that eight years earlier had cheered his debut century to the echo. It's probable that Warne's reception would have been still worse. He presented a bigger, richer and seemingly more vulgar target; Adelaidians, who reputedly thought Bradman something of an arriviste, never completely took to Warne anyway. Although he was to suffer financially from his misdemeanour, losing positions as a columnist at *The Age* and the *Daily Mirror*, being *hors de combat* during that Adelaide match may have been one of the luckier breaks of Warne's career.

The taint has never quite gone away. While no further information ever came to light about Warne in any of the several match-fixing investigations round the world, the effect of the spreading scandal was to blacken the reputation of everyone even peripherally involved. Every so often, a journalist will raise it, clasping ironic inverted commas around 'pitch and weather information'. Every so often, a talking head on one of those pugilistic Indian tabloid television shows will comment airily on Warne's nefarious associations, will remind his audience that there was a cover-up, will deplore that only players from the subcontinent ever get fingered for corruption.

Even Warne's public performance as a pundit is interpreted in the light that he once made private prognostications for 'John'. 'Should be a cracker,' Warne tweeted before India's game against England during 2011's World Cup. 'My prediction – a tie!' When it was, the Pakistan Cricket Board's voluble chairman Ijaz Butt and several former Pakistan players were quoted as demanding an ICC investigation. 'Genius or match-fixer?' asked the *Fox Sports* headline, insulated by a question mark from a colossal defamation.

And yet . . . and yet . . . the culture that had conduced to this crisis was to change. Codes of conduct were rewritten specifically to proscribe all contact with bookmakers, codes of behaviour altered so that casinos grew less popular for relaxation. The custom of appointing old buffers as Australian team managers was discontinued, the younger and abler Steve Bernard taking on a role that he continued for fifteen years. And against all odds, the organisation that under Malcolm Speed was about to become Cricket Australia embraced principles of transparency – well, less opacity anyway. Key reports began to be made public as a matter of course – commencing with the O'Regan report into match-fixing, which damned the Board for its cover-up. Damaging events were no longer to be hidden, as 24-year-old Ricky Ponting discovered after sustaining a vivid black eye in an altercation with a bouncer at the storied Sydney nightspot, the Bourbon & Beefsteak. Six weeks after Warne and Waugh had made their halting and restricted appearances in front of the media at the Adelaide Oval, Ponting had to bear the mark of his disgrace at a press conference at his Hobart home ground while his teammates took the field without him, and to answer questions about how he intended to overcome his 'problem with alcohol'.

Ponting's immediate three-match suspension sent out a strong message: the system will no longer protect you. Shane Warne, then, could be regarded as an agent of change – albeit an agent of change who for his own part remained quite unaltered.

Fundamental to the establishment of Warne as cricket's human headline was *where* he played. Warne's arrival in England in 1993 coincided with a bullish, post-Wapping, pre-Leveson era on Fleet Street, with circulations and salaries still rising, and the internet and social media yet to intrude. To the inheritors of the mantle of *Scoop*'s Shumble, Whelper, Pigge and Corker, Warne was a story waiting to happen, the absolute embodiment of the proverbially gormless Aussie: a blond-haired, bold-faced mix of sportsman, soapie star and beach bum, who could have walked off the set of *Neighbours*, and who once bitten was never shy. England's newspaper culture was far more carnivorous than Australia's, where Warne was for the moment still regarded chiefly as a sportsman, and treated accordingly with a certain deference and restraint – at least as yet.

What really happened to Warne was that he suffered the worst of both worlds. The usual pattern of a Warne misdemeanour started with a revelation in an English red top, where it was a sensation for a day before journalists moved on; it would then run for weeks in Australia, sustained by the censorious opinionistas, voluble shock jocks and television current-affairs ambulance chasers in which the country had begun to abound. In England, Warne was one of a host of potential providers of tabloid fodder; in Australia, he had few competitors when it came to subjects it was fun to prognosticate and moralise about. This led Warne, interestingly, to think that he received a squarer deal abroad than at home: 'The English media treated me so much better than the Australian press.' Fleet Street used to catch him out, thought Warne, but at least they didn't go on and on about it. In fact, it was the media in each country at its worst: England at its most voyeuristic and prurient, Australia at its most trivial and prim, in synergistic relation.

Which brings us to the ladies. Perhaps you remember some of them. There was the 'exotic dancer'. There was the 'hairy-backed sheila'. There was the 'stunning blonde promotions model'. There was a girl with whom he had sex on the bonnet of his car who then took the tabloid shilling. There were the girls with the sex toys with whom he cavorted in his Playboy underpants whilst being recorded by a hidden camera. A fair proportion of any A–Z of Warne would have to be devoted to distinguishing the many young and also not-so-young women who revealed themselves publicly as notches on Warne's bedpost, before, during and after his twelve-year marriage to Simone. The mother of Warne's three children proved to be a woman of staggering resilience, and Warne a husband of proportional bouncebackability.

At the end of that delicious sports movie *Slap Shot*, the Charlestown Chiefs hockey team's irrepressible bum of a coach, Reggie Dunlop (Paul Newman), tells the estranged wife he still loves that he's under offer from the Minnesota Nighthawks. His wife knows that he is a hopeless case, a bed-hopping boyo, full of naïve exuberance and superficial charm. She shakes her head noncommittally and walks away. 'So?' says another character. 'Is she coming to Minnesota?' Reg smiles: 'Oh, for sure.' Warne must have been possessed of similar self-confidence.

The costliest and most humiliating of Warne's peccadilloes involved a 22-year-old nurse, Donna Wright, whom Warne, after a county match for Hampshire, met at a Leicester nightclub in 2000. Although she declined an invitation back to his room at the Leicester Holiday Inn, Warne later drunkenly plied her with lewd voice messages, the parts of which that weren't censored worming their way into the *Daily Mirror* beneath the headline 'SHAME WARNE'. It painted an excruciating portrait of a married thirty-year-old behaving like a horny teenager. And it was, as most such stories would be in England, gone in an instant, the *Mirror* moving on to its next *succès de scandale,* Ally McCoist, Dwight Yorke or whoever, without missing a beat.

The story echoed longer and louder in Australia, reverberating round talkback radio, on op-ed pages, and in the boardroom at Cricket Australia, which had once sized Warne up for the captaincy of Australia, and quite possibly would be called on to do so again.

Via his manager Austin Robertson, Warne received an invitation from Channel Nine's *A Current Affair* to make 'an apology' on air to his wife, family and public. Warne complied, albeit reluctantly, and during the interview with Mike Munro exuded an aura of impenitence: he had thought it was a 'private matter'. 'I didn't think it was going to become public, and now that it has become public I suppose it's a mistake,' he said. 'If it had stayed private it wasn't a mistake.'

Warne was pilloried for his lack of obvious contrition. In *Spun Out,* Paul Barry lays it on with customary thickness: 'So how on earth could Shane get it so wrong, both with Simone and the public?' But in doing so, Barry conflates two different questions. Warne's accountability to his wife and to the public were not remotely the same thing. Warne had assuredly been beastly to his wife; to Donna Wright too, to a lesser degree. But exactly what was the public's place in all this? Was there *really* a public clamour for an act of apology? Or was it simply another example of the media's seldom-examined assumption that it genuinely reflects at all times what the public believes and is interested in?

Funnily enough, liberal opinion would generally categorise *A Current Affair* as a boneheaded parody of current-affairs journalism, full of feigned concern and phoney empathy, involved in the headlong pursuit of ratings and nothing else. And surely that is exactly the role it was performing here, following up a one-day wonder in a tabloid newspaper on the other side of world with a contrived chunk of ratings bait. Which of these on-set reactions sounds likelier? 'Tonight, colleagues, we serve the nation by performing the solemn duty of holding a widely admired Australian to account for his actions', or 'We've got Warnie! *Today Tonight* doesn't! This'll rate through the roof.'

So why should Warne have participated in such a cynical exercise? Arguably, his mistake was not in failing to offer a public apology, but in appearing at all, signing up to the cycle of commodified sin and redemption in which the media so willingly wallows. Barry argues that Warne's obduracy showed that 'his life had become so unreal he had lost his bearings' and 'he no longer knew how ordinary people lived or thought'. But, frankly, Warne's position seems closer in conception to everyday attitudes: that what happens in a marriage is for the partners to work out between themselves, and does not require colluding in tabloid television's fantasies about itself as arbiter of moral behaviour.

Warne's concluding remark on *A Current Affair* – that 'if it had stayed private it wasn't a mistake' – was hardly likely to engender widespread public sympathy; nor did it suggest a highly developed conscience. In a brutally practical sense, though, it was true. Warne had behaved obnoxiously, but the media's fascination was with the perpetrator of the offence rather than its nature: they were interested in Warne's embarrassment, not in mounting a campaign for improved nightclub etiquette. More intelligent individuals than Warne have echoed his argument that 'what's private should stay that way'; the famous nostrum that Bill Clinton imparted to Monica Lewinsky was that 'if two people say something didn't happen, then it didn't happen'. And not only did a host of distinguished thinkers enlist to argue that Clinton's private life was nobody's business save his own, but the public were also persuaded, re-electing the Democrats in the mid-term elections afterwards with an increased number of seats.

Warne actually paid a comparatively heavier price for his mis-demeanour than America's priapic president. Clinton kept his job and preserved his marriage. Warne lost his job at once. Although he had been representing Hampshire and not Australia at the time, Warne's commission as national vice-captain was revoked at the start of August 2000. Warne was dumbfounded: 'I couldn't believe it was happening. It was a mistake, yes, but it was a private matter and had nothing to do with cricket. Explicit talk on the telephone did not mean all of a sudden I'd lost my flipper or forgotten how to set a field.'

Barry cites this as further evidence that Warne was living in cloud-cuckoo-land, ascribing to him the 'bizarre view' that the Board 'should have stamped on any journalist who dared link the scandal to his role as captain'. Actually, it's not clear that Warne was calling for any stamping at all. He was simply pointing out that his behaviour in nightclubs, no matter how unpleasant, and his marital fidelity, no matter how contingent, did not bear directly on his cricket expertise, or his competence as a captain. What exactly were the off-field responsibilities of a senior Australian cricketer, and where were they spelled out? Were we really more constipated than the English, with their reverence for George Best ('I spent 90% of my money on drink and women. The rest I wasted') and Frank Worthington ('I managed to seduce a Swedish teenager and her mother. They were great days'), and the Americans, still pleased to exalt Wilt Chamberlain ('I was just doing what was natural – chasing good-looking ladies, whoever they were and wherever they were available', which apparently happened 20 000 times)?

To be fair to the directors of Cricket Australia who stripped Warne of office, their concern was not so much with the Donna Wright affair than with what they might wake up to one morning with Warne in the big job. They had some basis for thinking that way. Warne had had a highly visible six months leading up to the *Mirror* exposé. Cricket Australia had accepted Warne's protestations of innocence when Scott Muller was audibly derided on Nine's coverage of the Bellerive Oval Test in December 1999, and taken no disciplinary action against him for clashing with two fifteen-year-olds who had taken his photograph while he was smoking at Westpac Stadium in Wellington. With each episode, CA's directors experienced premonitions of future risks where Warne was involved. Warne kind of it knew it too.

A few weeks after the *Mirror* exposé, Warne and Robertson met at the Royal Garden Hotel in London with Speed, who gave Warne a thick bound copy of reports on the Wright affair from the Australian press. As Speed and Robertson discussed various business issues, Warne flicked through the pages seriously, perhaps struck by the weightiness of the tome. 'I've decided,' he said at last. 'I am going to give up my rooting.' Speed turned to Robertson. 'Do you think he could do that, mate?' The laconic Robertson knew his man. 'Not a chance,' he replied.

But it was not only Warne's nocturnal trysts that deprived him of the chance to captain Australia. Some boosters, including his staunch advocate Ian Chappell, have projected Warne into the role of the modern Keith Miller, proverbially 'the best captain Australia never had', who missed his opportunity because the narcs and straiteners of the 1950s disapproved of his racy lifestyle. There's something to this vision of Miller, but not much to this vision of Warne. For one thing, it's difficult to argue that Mark Taylor, Steve Waugh and Ricky Ponting as alternatives to Warne were as inferior as Ian Johnson and Ian Craig were to Miller; for another thing, it was Warne's misfortune that, at the points the captaincy torch was passed, he was scarcely in contention. When Waugh succeeded Taylor, it was not clear that Warne would be seen again as a cricket force; when Ponting succeeded Waugh, it was not clear he would even be seen again at all. This brings us to the third controversy – the costliest of all.

Warne began the summer of 2002–3 looking as taut and terrific as he ever had, a veritable Chesty Bond: if the frequency with which he was photographed at training with his shirt off was anything to go by, he knew it too. Warne's battles with his weight had been many and public: five years earlier, he had walked out of a press conference promoting a model of him that appeared in a Madame Tussauds exhibition after a journalist made a crack about his avoirdupois. Now he was showing off a physique embodying a six-pack rather than suggesting the other sort.

That new nimbleness tempted him to feats of athleticism, and during a VB Series match on 15 December 2002 he landed on his shoulder in diving to his right to intercept a drive down the on side of the pitch. The resultant dislocation jeopardised his chance to play a part defending the World Cup in South

Africa. Nonetheless, five weeks later, he called together a press conference to announce that he would be back to make the Cup his one-day swansong. He still looked a treat, too – too much so, as it proved.

Cricket Australia had for the previous couple of years been following protocols of the Australian Sports Drug Agency. Domestic and international players were subjected to regular screenings. On 10 February 2003, the day before Australia began their Cup defence against Pakistan at New Wanderers, Warne was alerted at Johannesburg's Sandton Sun hotel to the fact that urine he'd passed nineteen days earlier had revealed traces of hydrochlorothiazide and amiloride: diuretics known for their use in the masking of steroids. Next in the Australian camp to know were team doctor Trefor James and physiotherapist Errol Alcott, who shared the news with their team's new captain Ricky Ponting. 'One of the biggest stories in world cricket is about to break,' Alcott told him without fear of contradiction.

Confession having worked eight years earlier where his contact with 'John' was concerned, Warne owned up: to shed a little excess padding he had taken what he called a 'fluid tablet' called Moduretic recommended by his mother Brigitte. But times had changed. Partly because of the criticism of Cricket Australia's lenience towards Warne and Waugh four years earlier, this could not be swept away: Warne would be heading home for a hearing of a three-member anti-doping policy committee. And Ponting, the first cricketer to have borne the brunt of that new openness, post his night at the Bourbon & Beefsteak, was not unqualified in his sympathy: 'Every year we have a lecture on drugs, and I know I understand the issues well enough to check everything I take with either Hooter [Alcott] or TJ [James] before I take it. That is common sense and for Warnie, who has been playing international cricket for a decade, to ignore that approach is just madness.'

At 6 pm, manager Steve Bernard opened a team meeting in his room: 'Warnie has got something to say to us all.' A distressed and tearful Warne haltingly admitted taking his pill. 'Most of the players, if not all, have never seen Shane get so emotional that he cannot speak,' wrote Glenn McGrath in his diary. 'But tonight there is a deathly silence in the room.' Ponting broke the spell: 'OK, it's 6 o'clock. Go and have dinner, talk amongst yourselves, get over it. Come back at 9 and erase it from your memory because we've got a game to win.' After Warne had recited a *mea culpa* at a press conference before play the next day, Australia did, opening what would be an undefeated campaign in style.

By the time he landed in Melbourne, Warne had convinced himself that he could escape serious consequences, insisting that he was 'hopeful of returning back to South Africa to play a part in the World Cup'. He called people he thought could help, including Kerry Packer, and tried to rally the media, *The Australian* divulging Brigitte's role publicly. She, the paper reported, had pestered Warne into taking the tablet in order that he might look his best for the press conference foreshadowing his one-day retirement. 'For Christ's sake, just give me the tablet,' it quoted Warne as saying.

But there was to be no remission. Although the panel refrained from imposing the maximum sentence of a two-year ban because the urine had contained no steroid residue, it docked Warne a year of his time for a 'reckless act totally disregarding the possible consequences', and condemned what it called 'vague, inconsistent and unsatisfactory' testimony that made it difficult to 'accept that he was entirely truthful'. In particular, it emerged that traces of a diuretic had shown up in a test back in December, suggesting that a second tablet had been involved.

In one of those quirky Warnian paradoxes, it was his testimony's vague, inconsistent unsatisfactoriness that made it credible. The Warne explanation that fits snugly together, that doesn't shift ground, doesn't add detail along the way as it comes to mind and is not strewn with excuses will be the one to disbelieve, the one we will know is contrived and rehearsed. While he pays unconscious homage to Saki's dictum that 'a little inaccuracy sometimes saves tons of explanation', Warne is not a practised or elaborate liar, because he is not very good at it. Nor was admitting that he was so sensitive about his weight at the age of thirty-three that he did what his mother told him something done lightly.

What cost Warne instead was his brazenness. If the *Current Affair* interview with Mike Munro thirty months earlier had been understandably self-protecting, this one with Ray Martin was utterly self-serving: no, he hadn't paid any attention to the lectures about banned substances, 'the same as when I was at school'; no, he wasn't vain, merely proud of his appearance, and he'd 'earned that'. This 'innocent mishap' was peripheral stuff, and he was all about the main game: 'Whether, rightly or wrongly, mate, whether you hate me, you like me, you love the way I play or whatever, the facts of the matter are that I don't read much, I don't take a lot of interest in the outside world . . . I just play cricket.'

But this *was* about playing cricket. While fans were prepared to accept that Warne's marriage was his own affair, this offence concerned his bond of good faith with them. Where his home life was concerned, Warne had asked to be treated like everyone else; this time, he was asking to be treated as someone different, to whom normal conventions should not apply. It takes effort to fuss Australians about doping; doping is something athletes from other countries do. But despite all the bonhomie between Warne and Martin, 60 per cent of the respondents to a viewer poll at the end of the show thought that Warne deserved to do the time, having done the crime.

Those who observed the rules, not surprisingly, took exception to Warne's stance. Asked in South Africa whether Warne was guilty of naïvety, Ponting replied cuttingly: 'For sure, or stupidity, one of the two.' The single pill that multiplied was bitter for Adam Gilchrist to swallow, and he remarked coolly in a newspaper column: 'I think there's no doubt people don't like being deceived.' The comment enraged Warne, who sent word via Steve Bernard that he now hated Gilchrist's guts and would never speak to him again. But Warne had also to face that the offence had cost him something he valued more than money, more than time, more than popularity – it had cost him esteem within the playing group. And where only injury had previously forced him to the wayside, now he had been incapacitated by a self-inflicted wound. In the wee hours of the morning in Melbourne, as Australia fought out a tight Test in the Caribbean in May 2003, Victorian keeper Darren Berry was surprised to receive a text message from his old teammate: 'I'm really missing it now mate.' It is a haunting image: deep in his big silent Brighton mansion, Warne was counting his losses as Australia extended its gains.

Perhaps Warne had expected a public outcry on his behalf. If so, he was disappointed. Australians might love their sport, adulate their athletes, and at times have trouble focusing on the bane of performance-enhancing drugs, but they also have a simple, unblinking, sometimes unthinking, respect for rules. And sport everywhere was belatedly but growingly earnest about its drug protocols: later in the year, Manchester United's Rio Ferdinand, a sportsman with an even higher profile than Warne's, was banned for eight months simply for missing a drug test. Australian cricketers would be furious a couple of years later when the Pakistan Cricket Board blithely waived the convictions of Shoaib Akhtar and Mohammad Asif for testing positive to the steroid nandrolone. 'It's a laughable point amongst our players because we've worked very hard to be clean athletes,' said Matthew Hayden. 'It's ludicrous and it's not fair. We're all tested equally.' Australians haven't always spoken out on such issues with moral ground beneath them, but the example of Warne had in this instance made it solid.

As we have seen, the suspension proved a baggy green blessing in diuretic disguise, for the last three years of Warne's career were as glorious as the rest, and as colourful. But the controversies were now sideshows rather than floorshows. Warne was now no longer playing one-day internationals, and never appeared in T20 internationals, so would be gone as soon as the five-day legs of tours were concluded; he actually spent less time representing Australia than he did Hampshire. With Ponting firmly in his role as captain, Warne's Test colleagues scarcely cared that he marched to the beat of a different drum, for his value to the band was inestimable. But henceforward his personal relationships in the Australian team were more of convenience than confraternity. More of his teammates were married, more of them travelled with spouses and offspring, more of them agreed with Steve Waugh that they were happier doing so.

Warne was married too, of course, although not for much longer, and when his relationship at last came unglued during the 2005 Ashes tour there was actually not as much company for him as there once might have been. He leaned in this time of trial not on one of his older comrades, but one of the newest – in fact, the team's second-youngest player.

I put on a brave face in public but when my hotel room door was shut I wasn't too good. I got upset looking at photos of my kids, just wishing they were still around. Michael Clarke was a big help. I felt a bit for 'Pup' as I offloaded all my troubles on to him, at a time in his life when he was trying to establish himself in the side and had his own issues. But he is my closest friend and mateship is the most important thing in life and he was there for me and I won't forget that, I really appreciated it. He spent hours with me, listening when I wanted to get something off my chest. I remember one night later in the tour when the two of us sat in the corner of a bar both pouring our hearts out. After a few pints and a few more vodka Red Bulls I think I said that I loved him. Jeez we were poleaxed that night.

It is an unconsciously revelatory passage: his 'closest friend' was someone he had played a dozen Tests with when there were those with whom he had played more than a hundred. It also sounds less like mateship than what we might call 'greatship' – the reverence of the protégé for the master rather than a relationship of equals. Warne was the still point in a cricket world that had drifted away from him.

Yet strangely, I suspect, it was precisely this drift that helped Warne make peace with the game, to tidy his loose ends, to know when his race was run, and when the moment was ripe for him to go to Ponting, after the Perth Test of 2006, and say: 'It's my time.'

Retirement has become a bizarrely divisive issue in recent years: witness the almost schismatic debates in India about whether senior players have 'earned the right' to 'go out on their own terms'; witness the distasteful death watches on Australian players felt to be in the home stretches of their careers. Warne's Test retirement was perhaps the least controversial act of his cricket life. There was little speculation leading up to it, little handwringing afterwards, and while it became a huge deal between times nobody seemed to think it was other than right, especially given the symmetry with the retirement of Glenn McGrath.

For the professional sportsman whose life has been so consumed by their career, retirement can seem like a kind of living death, or suspended animation. On her farewell in 2003, Cathy Freeman described her future as stretching out before her 'like a wilderness'. Steve Waugh's autobiography ends on the final day of his final Test, as though he was of interest only while playing, even to himself. Warne? He was only giving up cricket. He was not giving up being Shane Warne.

An underlying question in all recitations of Warne's misdemeanours is: how on earth did he endure them? Because not once was one ever able to say with confidence that his cricket was affected by the scrapes he experienced, the corners he found himself pushed into. The *Courier-Mail*'s Robert Craddock has given a fascinating eyewitness account of Warne's first exposure to a tabloid gotcha: a 1993 *Daily Mirror* interview with an ex-girlfriend from his time playing in the Lancashire League, which claimed he was possessive, publicly embarrassing, and not so 'hot in bed' anyway.

> Shane Warne walked into the breakfast room at London's Westbury Hotel and found his private life on toast. London's *Daily Mirror* had paid one of Warne's girlfriends from his old English league cricket days to reveal private love letters penned from the hand which would later rock the cricket world.
>
> It was mildly embarrassing stuff – particularly as Warne's girlfriend and future wife Simone had just arrived in town – and several chuckling teammates loitered at breakfast for the precious moment when their wide-eyed young teammate opened the papers and saw a saucy letter he had written two years before.

Warne, on his first Ashes tour and the brightest young prospect in world cricket, saw the story, momentarily stopped chewing his breakfast and read the entire piece without any conspicuous display of emotion. His subdued demeanour was no different to an investor seeing his stocks had dropped a point or two overnight. Then he calmly resumed his breakfast, and headed off to scalp England in the second Test with a four-wicket haul at Lord's a few hours later.

It was a habit to last a lifetime. On his last Ashes tour twelve years later, when he was never off the tabloid front pages, and keeping maudlin company with Michael Clarke, Warne bowled better and better with each passing Test. Barmy Army chants of 'Where's your missus gone?' gave way to stupefied choruses of 'We wish you were English.' Even John Buchanan was impressed enough to ask Warne how he managed it.

Shane simply said that the key to performing on the field was to arrive at the ground 'fresh and relaxed'. He told me no matter what else was happening in his life, he could close the door on it and arrive at a cricket ground 'fresh and relaxed' and ready to play. And whatever it took to close the door on an element of his life, he would do. Regardless of how it impacted on another person, so long as he felt he had closure, then he was able to arrive mentally fresh for cricket.

Buchanan thought this an 'amazing skill', and it is, although it is also perfectly explicable. Who has not taken up a pursuit as a consolation in time of trial? Who has not plunged themselves into work when under personal stress? Warne happens to have been better at his work than almost any of us will be at ours, and to have always obtained enormous gratification and acclaim from it. To have sought out the sense of mastery it gave him over his immediate environment, then, seems to me to be the most natural act in the world; it was a safe place to be, a bordered reality, a personal retreat. You could even go all Rumsfeldian and see the cricket field as the arena of 'known unknowns', the sometimes enchanting, occasionally forbidding but always finite possibilities of a day's play, and the rest of his human relations as full of 'unknown knowns', what Warne kept from others and from himself.

Warne is perhaps a little unusual in always seeming so ready to be famous, so comfortable with the limelight, so accepting of reading about, talking about and watching himself. But once habituated to attention, he apparently shared the sensations of Andre Agassi, who said that what struck him about fame was how normal it was: 'I marvel at how unexciting it is to be famous, how mundane famous people are. They're confused, uncertain, insecure, and often hate what they do. It's something we always hear – like that old adage that money can't buy happiness – but we never believe it until we see it for ourselves.' Warne was luckier than most, in that he loved what he did. And no wonder: it was always there for him.

FIVE

THE SPORT OF WARNE

AUSTRALIANS tend to regard themselves as uniquely passionate about sport. Whether a country of 21 million can truly be said to rival, say, the cricket culture of India or the football culture of Brazil or Italy is a moot point; this is not a matter of comparison but a form of definition, in which the passion is reinforced by a passion about the passion, watching ourselves watching sport being part of the experience, and the language we use expressing pathology rather than mere partiality: one is a 'mad football fan'; one is a 'golf nut'; one is a 'fanatical punter'; one is, of course, a 'cricket tragic'. Of the arts, literature and music, of course, one is always, far more tastefully, an aficionado, connoisseur or devotee.

What is certainly true is that Australian sport serves a host of social purposes. We are a big country thinly populated: sport brings us together in great numbers and for common ends. We are a wealthy country less equal than it fancies: sport has an abiding democratic appeal, bringing bluebloods and battlers together in ostensible parity. We are a country remote from the rest of the world: global sporting success provides us with heady draughts of reinforcement, a sense that other nations are paying attention to us, at least for a moment. We are a country short on civic awareness: local sport is an underappreciated contributor to inculcating practices of citizenship, bonds with community, respect for rules.

No wonder, then, that there remains truth in Donald Horne's remark that 'it is only in sport that many Australians express those approaches to life that are un-Australian if expressed in any other connection'. Sport is not life. Sport is better than life. Life is big, messy, confusing, contingent, compelling us to make decisions on the basis of imperfect information with finite resources, with no certainty about their outcome and no expectation of immediate resolution. Sport is bordered, unambiguous, unadulterated, meritocratic; it offers us simple questions, unqualified answers, straight lines, exact quantifications, winners and losers, heroes and villains. Or so we can pretend, when it is served up to us in the superficial, black-and-white terms in which it is usually consumed in this country.

That being so, sport in Australia is also a tide to stand against. A solid core of Australians is vexed by sport's popular accessibility, by its easy fit with our conformist and materialist sensibilities, by its alleged discouragement of intellectual effort. Sport 'addled the

Australian consciousness', complained Patrick White: 'This passion for perpetual motion – is it perhaps for fear that we may have to sit down and face reality if we don't keep going?' A hardy staple of op-ed pages everywhere is the 'why oh why' column complaining that Australia spends too much time exalting dumb athletes and not enough celebrating cutting-edge creative artists, as though it is a zero-sum game and a country can only do one at a time, as though athletes are non-creative and unartistic and artists not competitive and ambitious. While they like to think of themselves as hardy and independent, too, Australians are anxious about the world's good opinion, while aspiring to the 'relaxed erectness of carriage' that A.A. Phillips saw as an antidote to the 'cultural cringe'.

All of which positioned Shane Warne, assuredly relaxed if sometimes too erect for comfort, far closer to the centre of Australian life than a comparable athlete in another country, his achievements attaining greater cachet and his comportment exciting broader execration. So how, then, did Warne's career and life intersect with those three overlapping contested zones in our national sporting life: professionalism, aggression and masculinity?

Few words in the sporting lexicon are so rich in nuance as 'professional'. It conveys the highest praise: preparation, discipline, efficiency and effectiveness. It also has connotations of selfishness, uniformity, negativity and avarice. In Australian sporting terminology, 'professional' takes on additional dimensions. We have traditionally promoted 'natural' talent, while also believing in total subordination to collective goals. We have deplored the idea of our athletes turning into automata, while always wishing them to be 'good team men'. We have been happy to see them make loads of money, while holding fast to a conviction that they must be driven by a love of the game. We are advocates of progress and growth, nonetheless inclined to reveries about the gentler times and freer spirits of bygone days. While in other respects being very much a man of his time, even Shane Warne grows rheumy-eyed about the past, in his identification with the cricketers of the 1970s.

Warne's imaginings of that idyll are nostalgically selective. The Chappell era appeals to Warne, of course, in its seeming freedom from killjoy coaches, invasive inquisitors and pharisaical moralists, in its apparent licence to eat, drink and be merry unencumbered. But, as observed earlier, the deprivations of the era would hardly have appealed to him: the poor money, the minimal reinforcement, the need for self-mastery and self-direction. Cricket found him, to repeat his favourite incantation one last time, and it found him whilst searching. Terry Jenner did not bump into Warne in the street. Ian Chappell did not meet Warne at the pub. Pulling Warne up by his bootstraps was, at the critical early stage, a collective effort.

Warne was even luckier to find a system still inchoate. He and genuine cricket professionalism are coevals: they grew up together, made adjustments for one another, and got on each other's cases too, holding an argument that endures. Warne has in a sense preserved a little corner of the professional game for the irrepressible talent, who in the face of prescription and regimentation will always be able to argue: 'But this is the way *Warnie* did it.' At the same time, for all that he followed his own lights, Warne *was* a hard and dedicated worker, apt to take boxes of balls into empty nets to whirl away on his own at a single stump, to watch videos of opponents beyond the point of boredom, and even at times to tackle his weight by self-denial and self-mortification, grasping and coping with the changing capabilities of his physical mechanism as well as any cricketer in history. If he missed a team bus, it never got out. If he was at deviance from a team plan, it was never obvious. He never skipped a tour because he was tired, or bored, or indifferent. He never complained about 'the grind', or 'cricket lag', or 'burnout'. And, it must be said, he also adhered perfectly to the professional creed in cultivating very few outside interests.

Warne liked cars, golf and spending money. But when not playing cricket, he could be rather at a loss. Unlike others in his era who made the most of hiatuses to monetise their reputations, he was commercially haphazard. He mimicked Greg Norman with a range of wines. He followed Ian Healy into apparel with a range of underwear. The results were ho-hum. He was certainly nowhere near as conscientious as Steve Waugh, who announced the coming of each cricket season with his annual diary, and at the end poured his career out all over again into a two-kilogram autobiography; Warne's books by comparison were hurried and fragmentary. Part of it was undoubtedly idleness and indifference, money coming easily enough without his having to pursue it. Part of it, though, may have been a lack of confidence.

In the IQ stakes, Warne was hardly to be compared with Andrew Symonds, who once asked the name of 'that movie Jerry

Maguire was in', and what the 'RSPCA date' to Michael Kasprowicz's wedding was. Warne took exception when his captain Ricky Ponting used the word 'stupidity' about him in the context of his 2003 drug offence: 'Stupid's a harsh word, Ray. I don't consider myself stupid. I consider myself probably very silly, should have checked.' But when Jana Wendt interviewed him rather more perceptively three years later, she was struck by Warne's persistent use of the words 'stupid', 'dumb' and 'dummy' when talking about himself, and concluded that 'there is something gnawing at his sense of self when it comes to the subject of intelligence'.

And it was as though he did not quite trust his own judgement away from the playing field, preferring to follow others'. His first agent was his Victorian teammate David Emerson, who also managed Merv Hughes. He then followed his first captain, Allan Border, into the stables of Austin Robertson in Australia and Michael Cohen in the UK. He was managed for a period by his brother Jason – an arrangement that seemed to be more about protecting than promoting him. Not until 2005 did he finally gravitate towards the savvy James Erskine, and probably his highest-earning years have been *since* his retirement, when he has been a sought-after commentator, hair hawker, poker pusher, and domestic T20 gun-for-hire.

Funnily enough, Warne did not buy into the means by which the Australian cricket team subtly distanced itself from the idea it was simply a professional unit that went out and did a fair day's work for a fair day's pay. Warne has said that one of his proudest moments was looking up at the SCG's electronic scoreboard on his Test debut and seeing the welcome that announced him as 'Australia's 350th Test cricketer'; he also troubled to learn a little about cricket history after Terry Jenner's admonition: 'Test cricket didn't start in 1991, Shane. You did.' But about the baggy green cap he remained quietly agnostic. Except when required to, he did not wear it, and he was not one of the team's more-patriotic-than-thou exhibitionists, like Justin Langer, who kept it on for four days after 1997's Ashes were won, or Colin Miller, who had a baggy tattooed on his backside. Nor, unlike his pal Michael Clarke, did he call for it when in sight of his maiden Test hundred – considering that he holed out one short, maybe he should have.

The subtext is, of course, that the baggy green cult was tended most tenaciously by Steve Waugh, who once wore his at Wimbledon, and derided most scornfully by Ian Chappell, who has scoffed that he does not 'remember having one discussion about the cap during my playing days'. Warne's lèse-majesté has been used against him by, among others, Adam Gilchrist, who responded rather priggishly in December 2007 when Warne was quoted dismissing John Buchanan's contribution to the Australian ascendancy: 'I guess one of the traits that we have a lot of pride in, in wearing the baggy green, is that we show a lot of respect. It seems some guys in retirement have lost that . . . [The Australian team] is an elite club and we've always felt a major characteristic of being in that club is to show respect.'

Quite why Waugh reinforced his captaincy with so many props and symbols is an intriguing psychological question. Some saw it as self-promotion; a personal suspicion is that Waugh coveted the captaincy before quite grasping what it entailed, and as a self-contained man found it at first an uneasy fit. The activities and artefacts with which he surrounded his leadership were a means of distributing the burden; he could thereby make himself less an individual, more the representative of a lineage.

Waugh was famous for his diaries and his photographs. Both can act as a means of ordering and controlling experiences, putting a comforting distance between the act and the observer. Sport, of course, is replete with ego, and Waugh could not have competed without a sizeable one. But his wife Lynette, who writes as perceptively of her husband as anyone, has noted: 'Stephen has never – even as a baby, I'm told – liked a lot of attention.' And it's telling, I think, how swiftly and completely Waugh has receded in public consciousness since that final, rather fevered farewell in January 2004.

Shane Warne needed no symbols, no props, no enhancements. He simply went out and let the competitive juices flow – sometimes, it was felt, to a fault.

A few years ago, an Australian sporting myth was punctured in a way you would have to have been of stone not to draw a smile from. It concerned what has become known as 'The Gladiators': the image, captured by photographer John O'Gready, of diminutive Western Suburbs five-eighth Arthur Summons and towering St George forward Norm Provan, mummified in mud, seemingly on the point of a chivalrous embrace at the end of the 1963 New South Wales Rugby League grand final, in which the Dragons triumphed. More than forty years after the match, Summons and Provan were reunited on stage and asked to reminisce about their exchange.

What, Summons was asked, had he said to his lofty rival?

Said? What had he said? Summons would bloody tell you what he said: 'He wanted to swap jumpers and I told him to get stuffed and that St George not only beat us but the referee was paid to do a job on us. I told him I didn't want to swap my jumper with him and I didn't.'

Chuckles all round: it's been going on since Eve got into Adam about his aversion to apples, eh? Chalk one up for those who in the event of any antagonism on the sporting field say that it has always been there, that the old days ain't what they used to be, that the new ones aren't as bad as they're sometimes painted. It's an argument with which Shane Warne and the cricketers of his era would be thoroughly familiar, having been identified extensively with a kind of predatory Australian aggression that went under various guises, ranging from rudimentary 'sledging', a term in use since the 1960s for verbal commentary or abuse designed to distract or dismay an opponent, to the more sophisticated 'mental disintegration', which can be dated etymologically to Australia's 1989 Ashes tour – in fact, to a single dressing-room conversation, during the Sixth Test at the Oval.

This was the tour on which Allan Border made himself over, from mild-mannered introvert, prone to private losses of temper, to bloody-minded belligerent, maintaining a constant on-field growl between regular barks of anger. The context of the conversation was the timing of a declaration on the final day. When some players urged an early closure to maximise the chances of a 5–0 result, the Queenslander Carl Rackemann argued pithily that 'full mental and physical disintegration' would only result if Australia batted longer than England expected, forcing them into the demoralising state of bowling and fielding in futility. Border took this on board: after all, what had England done all summer to deserve a chance for a win? He deferred his closure until lunch on the last day, setting an impossible target of 393 in sixty-five overs that left England with nothing to play for – in the end, the Australians were thwarted only by bad light.

The phrase entered Steve Waugh's lexicon four years later when Border applied it at Headingley. Border and Waugh batted most of the second day in partnership, being 175 and 144 at the close respectively, but the former surprised the latter by batting almost another hour the next morning with the objective being to cause 'further mental and physical disintegration'. England slid quickly to three for 50, barely lasted the rest of the day, and were rounded up by an innings and 148 runs.

As originally intended, then, 'mental disintegration' was a rather more holistic approach to cricket than simply calling the opposition 'cunts'. It was about pushing your opposition beyond their limits, intimidating them with your relentlessness. There were a variety of non-verbal ways to do this: the bowler holding his line as the batsman ran through; the searing return just missing the batsman as he scurried for his ground; the general commitment to positive body language, which Warne himself was apt to preach the power of. 'When you turn up at a ground midway through a game it should be impossible to tell from the body language whether the fielding team is on top or behind,' he opined. 'You should have to look at the scoreboard, not see it in the field.' During Steve Waugh's captaincy, his informal guarantee of 400 runs a day was presented as a commitment to entertain, but it was to entertain right over the top of the opposition, casting them as the Washington Generals to the Australians' Harlem Globetrotters.

Used interchangeably, however, sledging and/or mental disintegration hallmarked Australian cricket in the country's great period of dominance – with the idea that Australia achieved some special advantage from being the biggest bully on the block. It had its apologists, such as Ian Chappell: 'A weakness of character is as legitimate a target as a weakness outside the off stump.' It had its spoof of the apologists too, such as Tom Gleisner's satiric creation Warwick Todd, who exclaimed that sledging, a venerable tradition, was 'as much a part of the game as ball-tampering and bribery'.

The sledging itself varied, naturally, in quantity and quality. It could be sly and wry, playing on an opponent's reputation, such as that for superstition of South African opening batsman Neil McKenzie, whose leg Adam Gilchrist liked to pull: 'You've stepped on a line, Neil!' It could be a nonstop cycle of rubbish, and usually was from Glenn McGrath, as once recorded by New Zealand's Adam Parore: 'You guys are shit. We can't wait to get rid of you so we don't have to play you. Get the Saffas over here so we can have a proper game of cricket. We can't be bothered playing against you. You're second raters.'

Warne was fluent in both varieties. 'Come on Ramps,' he chipped away at England's Mark Ramprakash during a tense session of the 2001 Trent Bridge Test. 'Use your feet and come down the wicket to me. You know you want to.' He drew the fatal indiscretion. Warne was also notoriously salty. 'Fucking arsey cunt,' his response to being hit for six by Stuart Carlisle in a VB Series match against Zimbabwe six months later, was classified by *Wisden Cricket Monthly* as the second-filthiest phrase attributed to a cricketer (ranking behind a line that John Emburey is said to have rendered, in his Peckham accent: 'The fackin' facker's fackin' facked'). The language was also famously constant, and pretty transparent in its purpose. Even a pretty poor batsman, such as the Englishman Matthew Hoggard, grasped what was going on.

Length ball, forward defensive, no run. 'Awww, fuck, jeez.' Widish ball outside off stump, left well alone, no run. 'Awww, fuck, jeez.' Fuller delivery turned into the leg side for single. 'Awww, fuck, jeez.' I thought he might have some sort of cricket Tourette's but Warnie knew what he was doing, creating an atmosphere around the batsman and attempting to chip away at his self-belief.

It wasn't, however, only about the batsman. From his first captain, Allan Border, Warne picked up the habit of stirring things up just to get a contest going. Particularly after 1989, Border thrived on a bit of toe-to-toe – with the bowler, with short leg, with the opposition captain or whoever was in earshot. He encouraged Warne to do the same: 'If things were not happening for me, he suggested, then it was probably worth having a word with the batsman – not for the sake of having a go, but to switch myself on for the contest.'

Warne was not indiscriminate in doing so. Because he was one himself, he recognised others who thrived on the contest. In a World Series Cup match at the SCG in January 1994, Warne dived to accept a low return catch from New Zealand's captain Ken Rutherford, a tough little scrapper who never took a backward step, and did not now – he would not budge, and the unsighted umpires had no choice but to reprieve him. Naturally enough, the Australians assailed him bitterly, which Rutherford rather relished, noting only that Warne remained aloof. Pumped up and chock-full of fight, Rutherford accosted Warne at the end of the over and asked if he had anything to add himself. 'No mate,' said Warne. 'I know you. If I did that it would only make you play better.'

When he sensed a vulnerability, however, he swooped, and unabashedly, as Adam Gilchrist relates in his autobiography. Warne and Gilchrist had first been teammates on the 1997 Ashes tour, then passengers on the same airliner home, Gilchrist having suffered a knee injury, Warne returning to Melbourne briefly for the birth of his first child: Gilchrist was touched that Warne sat with him in economy class when actually entitled to a first-class seat. They had played twenty-six one-day internationals for Australia together when they met on opposing sides in a Sheffield Shield match at the WACA in November 1998 – and Warne gave Gilchrist a right working over. 'You're an arse-licker,' snarled Warne when Gilchrist came in to bat. 'You've only got where you are because you're an arse-licker.' And so on, augmented by Warne's Victorian colleague Darren Berry, at great and repetitious length.

Yet this story merits some elaboration. At first glance, it appears simply an offensive way to deal with a sometime comrade, which is certainly the way Gilchrist took it: it was 'below the belt', 'extremely hurtful' and 'took a long time to heal'. When an upset Gilchrist later tackled him about it, Warne was bemused. 'We were only try-ing to upset you,' he laughed. They had succeeded, too: Gilchrist *was*, he had to admit, a 'conformist deep down', anxious to be well thought of. But there was also a sense in which this game probably got under Warne's skin too. It was his first first-class fixture since extensive shoulder surgery six months earlier; he was struggling on a ground at which he had never really succeeded, taking one for 74 from seventeen overs in a game that Victoria lost by 2 runs. This was an occasion, I sense, where the aggression possibly masked Warne's own vulnerability, thickly veiled as it usually was. Coincidentally or not, this was the only game in Warne's career after which he was publicly critical of the umpiring – for which he was fined.

Australian apologetics for sledging could be puerile. Some Australians, Warne included, tied themselves in moral knots trying to distinguish between themselves and rivals who retaliated, such as Arjuna Ranatunga, a canny cricketer with a talent for provocation, and Brian Lara, as fond as Warne of picking a fight to stimulate his competitive juices. Around Australian sledging, all the same, myth and legend accumulated. England's former captain Mike Atherton, whose Test experience encompassed the bulk of Warne's career, said that the most verbally aggressive Australian teams he encountered were at the very start of his career. After the advent of the ICC code of conduct and a few key retirements, such as Border and Hughes, he said, there was rather less than was often imagined.

Improved television coverage tended, meanwhile, to exaggerate what there was: one abrupt exchange picked up by a camera can by constant replaying become a war of words. It's arguable that the objection to Australian verbal aggression was as much about its context as its content, because it smacked of malicious glee, because it rubbed opponents' noses in Australian dominance. It may be telling that as an issue it has rather faded since the Australian team lost its top-dog mantle. There may be less of it; it may also be that it no longer sticks in craws as it used to.

For all his effing and blinding, too, Warne was often a notably generous opponent. At the end of his very first tour, to the West Indies with an Australian junior team in 1990, he was presented by a local official with a 'Friendship Award' for the freedom with which he had interacted with the opposition off the field, and it's probable that no cricketer of his era spent more time in rivals' dressing rooms. He took to certain players he just liked the spirit of – even Englishmen. During a mid-1990s form slump, Darren Gough received a fax of encouragement from Warne urging him to 'be natural, be yourself'. 'He'll do for me,' said Gough. Michael Vaughan has described going into the 2002–3 Ashes series resolved to play his strokes, getting himself out for 33 and 0 at the Gabba, and brooding afterwards until he ran into Warne. Good stuff, said Warne unbidden: he hadn't seen his mate McGrath tackled like that in ages; Vaughan should keep it up. Thus encouraged, Vaughan went on to a record-breaking summer.

Where opponents got the better of him, like Tendulkar and Lara, Warne was unfailingly generous, according them number one and two status in his *Shane Warne's Century*. Where he got the better of opponents, like Daryll Cullinan, he could be disarmingly charitable. Warne was the guest of honour at Cullinan's benefit dinner, where the South African has said 'he stole the show and was a great credit to the game'.

For probably the ugliest instance of Australian aggression in his era, and perhaps the historically most significant, Warne was nowhere in sight. This was a confrontation during the Fourth Test at St John's in May 2003 when Ramnaresh Sarwan had the temerity to respond to one of Glenn McGrath's trademark baits, and McGrath responded with a menacing spray including a threat to 'rip out' the batsman's throat. There were mitigations – including that McGrath was gravely concerned about the health of his cancer-stricken wife – but the public was not buying them. Steve Waugh later admitted he had seen the incident coming – observing, as he put it, 'the telltale signs that the kettle was on the boil'. But when it happened, he claimed to have been 'more concerned with organising a bowling change', and did nothing.

When the players gathered for a Cricket Australia function in Sydney a couple of months later, Waugh, McGrath, Ponting, Darren Lehmann and Matthew Hayden were shown footage of this and other recent incidents, watched an interview with a sponsor who admitted he was disturbed by the images, and an interview with the CA receptionist, who described being reduced to tears by fulminating members of the public. Out of a sobering meeting came Waugh's idea of committing players to a 'Spirit of Cricket' manifesto to 'make clear to everyone in the squad exactly what was acceptable, what wouldn't be tolerated and how we should carry ourselves' so that the team was 'remembered for all the right reasons' as a 'leader in all facets of the game'. The clauses headed 'our on-field behaviour' distinguished between 'positive play, pressure, body language and banter between opponents and ourselves', which it described as 'legitimate tactics and integral parts of the competitive nature of cricket', and 'sledging or any other conduct that constitutes personal abuse'.

Warne was not there, of course, because he was at the time serving his one-year ban from cricket for testing positive to a banned substance. One wonders how he would have responded to such a meeting; it might have been one of those in which he *did* pay attention. It's hard to imagine he would have been first to sign on. Airy invocations of the 'Spirit of Cricket' were everything he detested. He would have been even more irked by the clauses concerning 'our off-field behaviour', in which the Australian players agreed that this had 'the potential to reflect either positively or adversely on us as individuals and also on the game of cricket' and to 'warrant legitimate public criticism'. Because – phew! – this was a subject of which he had some first-hand experience.

In their 2006 interview, Jana Wendt put it to Warne that the 'final book' to be written about him would be divided three ways: the first part would be about 'sporting brilliance', the second about 'drama', and the third would be —

'Personal,' jumps in Warne.

'Women,' I say.

'Women, yeah,' says Warne, as if swallowing his medicine.

'Do you wonder about the way this particular chapter has had such a huge impact, not only on your private life, but on your public life – on how you're seen?'

'[On] my life, full stop. It has, but what do you do? I suppose you are who you are . . . I've got no-one else to blame about that stuff.'

True enough: he doesn't. But hang on: *a third* of an account of Warne's life would need to be devoted to his womanising? Aren't we getting it just a little out of proportion? Why is it our business? Who went to Warne for guidance in how to live one's life anyway? And how much do we *really* know? A great deal of Warne's reputation as a trouserman arises from that famously unimpeachable and not-at-all sex-obsessed source, the kiss-and-sell end of Britain's tabloid press. Many people who would regard themselves as discriminating and sceptical consumers of the media become strangely credulous when it reports on Warne. Because stories about sex are never exaggerated, are they? Because they're always related with absolute fidelity to the facts by entirely dispassionate people who aren't remotely influenced when they are offered money to retell them, isn't that right?

Here's my take, for what it's worth. Warne has been a philanderer, maybe even a compulsive one, although almost certainly a sentimental one, dedicated to the pursuit of poontang while at the same time exalting his wife, even after they were divorced. 'I'd like to thank her,' he said on his retirement, by which time they were. 'She's been my best friend for a long time.' Damien Fleming tells a story of waking up in the hotel room they were sharing to find Warne blubbing over the end of *Notting Hill*. You can imagine it, can't you? If only life were more like the movies. Warne's dedication to his three children, meanwhile, has always been touchingly absolute.

In August 2006, his Hampshire teammate Shaun Udal learned that his own son was autistic. The first person he bumped into was his Aussie skipper, in front of whom he burst into tears. Warne – 'a good man, a softer soul than the public perception', according to Udal – was immediately solicitous and helpful. 'I could not bear it if anything happened to my kids,' Warne said seriously. 'That is the one thing that has not happened to me.'

Warne actually used to put me in mind of Edward Ashburnham in Ford Madox Ford's *The Good Soldier*: charmingly shallow, good-natured, weak-willed, and 'positively revolted at the thought that she [his wife] should know the sort of thing that he did'. John Dowell, whose wife Ashburnham steals, nonetheless thinks him 'just a normal man' and develops a strange sympathy for him: 'He seems to me like a large elder brother who took me out on several excursions and did many dashing things whilst I just watched him robbing the orchards, from a distance.' Dowell even empathises with Ashburnham's impulses to deceive his nearest and dearest: 'In all matrimonial associations there is, I believe, one constant factor – a desire to deceive the person with whom one lives as to some weak spot in one's character or in one's career. For it is intolerable to live constantly with one human being who perceives one's small meannesses.'

Warne was hopeless – always getting caught, always resolving and dissolving, always making promises he was bound to break. Called on to express regret or contrition, he had the capacity to look even worse – bumbling, defiant, unprepared, uncomprehending. But in his hopelessness he was at least consistent. He did not live an elaborate lie like Tiger Woods. He did not manipulate as cynically as Ben Cousins. He did not sleep with his best friend and closest comrade's wife, like Wayne Carey. Perhaps due to a lack of the concentration and commitment to sustain it, there remained about him not an ounce of polish or pretension.

Ours has been a generation adept at letting ourselves off the hook. We may do bad things, but we're not bad people. It's our glands/genes/upbringing/society/drug of choice that made us do it. I dare say Warne tried all these on for size. He was lonely. He was far away. He'd had a drink. She threw herself at me. And it is naïve to ignore this last. The sexual revolution coincided with the beginnings of the globalisation of professional sport: sex was thus more freely available to sportsmen more widely celebrated. Montaigne observed that 'every man if his wishes and desires through life were chronicled would deserve hanging ten times over': the concupiscent male athlete and the amorous female groupie of the present generation have had more opportunity to indulge wish and desire, and perhaps been more protected from the risk of public hanging. Peter Brock's reputation as 'Peter Perfect', for example, was never jeopardised by a sexual prodigality to which colleagues and media turned a benign, unseeing eye, and which his wife Bev regarded with similar forbearance to Simone Warne's.

> I mean, what guy isn't going to feel chuffed when gorgeous women are hanging on his every move? . . . I had never had any doubt at all about Peter's love for me and the kids, but when life presents you with a constant, delectable everchanging smorgasbord, then it is difficult to always say 'no' and walk away . . . He often ventured out into new and exciting

territory, but he always kept coming back; after all, how many women was he likely to come across who would let him get away with as much as I did? Besides which, he did genuinely love me and showed it in the only way he knew how at the time.

Bev Brock might almost be channelling Warne himself when she adds: 'For a male, an affair is usually just that – a release of testosterone without there being much more to it.' Warne drew a similar distinction: 'I've never fallen in love with anyone [else]. I've never done any of that sort of stuff.'

One final comment: both sport and sex are *au fond* about physical confidence, even if we speak more freely about the sensuality in sport than the sport in sensuality. We are a society that accords social approbation to sexual prowess. That some members of a class of men and women whose lives revolve around competition and physicality should be drawn to achieving a sense of that reputation and self-estimation seems utterly unsurprising. In his autobiography, on the cover of which he smoulders like Fabio Lanzoni, Imran Khan explains that the turning point in his career was coming to England, where not only did the ball swing more but so could he. Imran confides improbably that he grew up with a complex about his looks, so adamantly did his older sister insist that he was ugly. 'It came as a pleasant surprise when I first began to be thought of as good-looking,' Imran says. 'I suspect that this coincided with my cricket success.' There it is, really: show me a heterosexual male who does not admit to feeling buoyed by an acknowledged attractiveness to women and I will show you a liar.

If we cannot know whether Warne sought sex out for his sporting ego's sake, it's scarcely an impossibility.

Hereabouts, though, we move into speculative territory. I have some expertise about Warne the cricketer, of whom I have seen much, but not much about Warne the person, with whom my relationship is comprehensively superficial. And, to be frank, that suits me fine. I only wished to watch him play cricket; I didn't want to marry him.

You're a long time retired, it is said, usually with a rueful intonation. Most athletes dwindle in their profile when their playing days expire. Not so long ago, Steve Waugh turned up in an advertisement for health insurance, instantly recognisable to some but requiring the elaborating caption 'Australian cricket legend' for others. That does not seem to be the case with Warne. Going on six years since he played his last Test, he remains Australian cricket's biggest box-office attraction, and has perhaps never been more successful or more sellable. One whose losses at the gaming table once led him into dubious company has become a professional casino habitué, Australia's poker ambassador. One whose relations with the sporting media were often ambivalent has become an accomplished member of it, a playful, knowledgeable and contagiously cheerful commentator. Not every great athlete makes the transition. Not every sports fan wants them to. David Foster Wallace once complained that listening to John McEnroe commentate was like watching William

Faulkner do a Gap advertisement. Warne has a knack of making it sound like you're standing in the catching cordon beside him, enjoying the occasion, chatting the day away.

Warne's most intriguing transition has been into a life beyond sport. Few athletes have slipped so easefully into the environs of fame populated by pop stars, movie stars, television personalities and supermodels. His permatanned features and Pepsodent smile testify to the properties of numerous unguents and preserving agents. His suddenly svelte physique advertises a new preference for protein shakes over toasted sandwiches. In his uninhibited Twitter slip-stream he drags along almost 850 000 followers, exhibiting remarkable capacities for continued news-making: when a cricket-related tweet hits a press box, the sight of reporters scurrying to collect responses is like watching a torchbeam scatter cockroaches in a darkened room.

Not everything to which he has turned his hand has succeeded. Perhaps the worst misadventure was *Warnie*, the stale, formulaic talk show in which Australia's greatest leg spinner was cast in the role of vernacular Michael Parkinson, and in which the result was probably a little more successful than if Parky took up leg spin; it topped at least one viewer poll as Australia's worst Australian television programme. Yet *Warnie* was a strangely telling experiment. Warne, who seems born to television, who has likened his life to a soap opera and refers to its superintending 'scriptwriter', was buried beneath his show's layers of production, contrivance and corniness: the exercise probably told you more about television than about Warne.

His Twitter stream, @warne888, seems somehow truer to Warne's nature – his spontaneity, his ingenuousness, his impetuousity, his utter everydayness, whether he is soliciting views about budgie-smugglers, mentioning his dreams featuring Scooby-Doo and his favourite characters in *Gilligan's Island*, or simply shooting the virtual breeze ('UNSTACKING DISHWASHER !!!!!!!!!!!!!!', 'How much does it hurt when you cut your finger nails to short !!!!' [sic]).

Sachin Tendulkar's Twitter stream soon petered out in the face of the unappeasable cravings of his two million followers. Warne keeps the faith with a rapt audience who cheerfully retweet everything from his philosophies of life to pictures of his son's Lego creations: packing his three children off on their new school years took four continuous tweets that would have struck a chord with any parent. Twitter helps Warne corral and control his fame, while also keeping him *au courant*.

Warne's stepping into life beyond sport was best actualised in May 2011 when he finally bid a fond adieu to the IPL at Wankhede Stadium and sauntered into the passionate public embrace of girl-friend Elizabeth Hurley, former squeeze of the actor Hugh Grant. What a transition: from Warnanmagrah to Warnieanliz, from a fixture of *Wisden* and *The Cricketer* to the stock-in-trade of *Hello!* and *OK!* Keith Miller and Princess Margaret was just a bit of tittle-tattle; Warne and Hurley have been grist for the tabloid mill since the very day they met in July 2010, when they were photographed flirting in the grandstand at the Glorious Goodwood festival by a *Daily Mail* paparazzo.

Hurley's birthplace of Basingstoke is known to cricket as the hometown of John Arlott – he of the rolling, throaty cadences. But when other English belles were abandoning their cut-glass vowels for estuary English in the 1980s, Hurley was converging on an accent that is the essence of posh, as distinct from Posh. Although *Vogue* once called her a textbook example of how to be famous without being successful, she has been in her way Britain's celebrity Olympian, ever avid for the big occasion, ever poised in clutch moments. 'She's good at it,' averred Clive James, that shrewd student of stardom. 'You won't get any Britney Spears moments from her.' First dismissed as a kind of animatronic clothes horse, she came into her own in the aftermath of Grant's infamous 1995 hooker misadventure on Sunset Boulevard. With the press and paparazzi laying siege outside, Hurley appeared at the front door of their London townhouse dressed in full Versace splendour, gorgeous makeup, vertiginous heels, voluptuous fur. Journalist Tom Sykes recalled her negotiating the footpath like a red carpet, 'smiling if not actually waving' as the flashbulbs popped, silencing the assembly with her poise. Only when she had driven off was the onlookers' reverie broken by the booming voice of a cockney photographer: 'Did not one of you useless c---s think to ask 'er a fucking question?'

Hurley is known to apply the expression 'civilians' to those outside the circles of fame – and in Warne, of course, she has paired up with a veteran combatant. Perhaps that understanding is a basis to their rapport. If so, it is a disarmingly positive and wholesome endorsement of fame. In economic terms, theirs seems a merger with synergistic benefits – in glamour, limelight, relevance and reputation. And who knows? They may even be happy together.

You would no more try to predict what Warne might do next than you would have tried to predict what he might bowl next:

his capacity to surprise has extended, after all, sometimes to himself. So far he has belied the assumption that the afterlives of athletes are invariably anticlimactic. But life should now be at least a little more predictable for him, if only because the daily variable of sporting fortunes has been removed from it: Texas hold 'em lacks the same thrill as Warnie bowled 'em. And the ground *has* subtly shifted. Now that the sheen of celebrity is on him, he is more interchangeable with others than he was. Now that the envelope of wealth has sealed around him, he is also less seemingly accessible. For those who've always seen him as a hedonistic boy-man from the suburbs who represents the most trivial and meretricious dimensions of the culture, there may be more coming to strengthen the impression. But if this man of comparatively few close friends and hundreds of millions of acquaintances is perhaps at risk of being swept away from us at last, then a word is due on what he has represented. Cricket is not after all *so* important; I'm bound to say that by several rigorous measures it may even be judged quite trivial. But being day in, day out for nearly two decades *the best at something that there has ever been* is assuredly not. To approach every day of that period with zest and zeal is to accomplish something worth celebrating.

In his classic essay on the fives champion John Cavanagh, William Hazlitt advised high culture not to dismiss low culture too airily, lest it draw attention to its own insignificances: 'It may be said that there are things of more importance than striking a ball against a wall—there are things, indeed, that make more noise and do as little good, such as making war and peace, making speeches and answering them, making verses and blotting them, making money and throwing it away. But the game of fives is what no one despises who has ever played at it.' In describing Cavanagh, the essayist invited his readers to consider not so much fives, or even sport, but mastery. 'He could do what he pleased, and he always knew exactly what to do,' wrote Hazlitt. 'He saw the whole game, and played it.'

Just like Warnie.

SOURCES

CRICKET

Atherton, Mike, *Opening Up*, Hodder & Stoughton, London, 2002

Barry, Paul, *Spun Out*, Bantam, London, 2006

Berry, Darren, *Keeping It Real: The Darren 'Chuck' Berry Story*, Bas, Melbourne, 2004

Border, Allan, *Beyond Ten Thousand: My Life Story*, Swan Publishing, Nedlands, 1993

Bryden, Colin, *Herschelle: A Biography*, Central, Johannesburg, 2003

Buchanan, John, *The Future of Cricket: The Rise of Twenty20*, Hardie Grant, Melbourne, 2009

Chappell, Ian (with Ashley Mallett), *Chappelli Speaks Out*, Allen & Unwin, Sydney, 2005

—— *A Golden Age*, Pan Macmillan, Sydney, 2006

Donald, Allan (with Pat Murphy), *White Lightning*, CollinsWillow, 2000

Dunne, Steve (with Brent Edwards), *Alone in the Middle: An Umpire's Story*, Penguin, Wellington, 2004

Emburey, John, *Spinning in a Fast World*, Robson, London, 1989

Gibbs, Barry, *My Cricket Journey*, Wakefield, Adelaide, 2001

Gilchrist, Adam, *True Colours*, Pan Macmillan, Sydney, 2009

Gillespie, Jason (with Lawrie Colliver), *Dizzy*, Harper Sorts, Sydney, 2007

Hayden, Matthew (with Robert Craddock), *Standing My Ground*, Penguin, Melbourne, 2011

Healy, Ian, *Hands & Heals*, Harper Sports, Sydney, 2000

Hoggard, Matthew, *Welcome to My World*, Harper Sports, London 2009

Hussain, Nasser (with Paul Newman), *Playing with Fire*, Penguin, London, 2005

James, C.L.R., *Beyond a Boundary*, Aurum, London, 2005

Jenner, Terry (with Ken Piesse), *TJ: Over the Top*, Information Australia, Melbourne, 1999

Knox, Malcolm, *The Greatest*, Hardie Grant, Melbourne, 2010

—— *Taylor and Beyond*, ABC Books, Sydney, 2000

Lee, Brett (with James Knight), *My Life*, Random House, Sydney, 2011

Murphy, Pat, *The Spinner's Turn*, Dent, London, 1982

Nyren, John, *The Young Cricketer's Tutor*, Davis-Poynter, London, 1974

Ponting, Ricky (with Brian Murgatroyd), *World Cup Diary 2003*, Hi Marketing, 2004

—— *The Captain's Diary 2005*, Harper Sports, Sydney, 2005

Ponting, Ricky (with Geoff Armstrong), *The Captain's Diary 2007*, Harper Sports, Sydney, 2007

Ray, Mark, *Border and Beyond*, ABC Books, Sydney, 1995

Rutherford, Ken, *A Hell of a Way to Make a Living*, Moa, Auckland, 1995

Ryan, Christian (editor), *Australia: Portrait of a Cricket Country*, Hardie Grant, Melbourne, 2011

Slater, Michael (with Jeff Apter), *Slats*, Random House, Sydney, 2005

Speed, Malcolm, *Sticky Wicket: A Decade of Change in the World of Cricket*, Harper, 2011

Taylor, Mark, *A Captain's Year*, Ironbark, Sydney, 1998

—— *Time to Declare*, Ironbark, Sydney, 1999

Trueman, Fred and Trevor Bailey, *The Spinner's Web*, Willow Books, London, 1988

Vaughan, Michael, *Time to Declare*, Hodder & Stoughton, London 2009

Warne, Shane, *My Own Story*, Swan Publishing, Sydney, 1997

—— *My Autobiography*, Hodder & Stoughton, London, 2001

—— *My Official Illustrated Career*, Cassell, London, 2006

—— *Shane Warne's Century: My Top 100 Test Cricketers*, Mainstream, London, 2008

Watson, Shane, *Watto*, Allen & Unwin, Sydney, 2011

Waugh, Steve, *Ashes Diary*, Harper Sports, Sydney, 1997

—— *Ashes Diary*, Pan Macmillan, Sydney, 1993

—— *No Regrets: A Captain's Diary*, Harper Sports, Sydney, 1999

—— *Out of My Comfort Zone*, Penguin, 2005

—— *Steve Waugh's South African Tour Diary*, Pan Macmillan, Chippendale, 1994

—— *Never Say Die*, Harper Sports, Sydney, 2003

Wendt, Jana, 'Shane Warne: Behind the Shades', *The Bulletin*, 14 March 2006

Wilde, Simon, *Shane Warne: Portrait of a Flawed Genius*, John Murray, London, 2007

OTHER

Agassi, Andre, *Open: An Autobiography*, Vintage, London, 2010

Anonymous, *Primary Colors: A Novel of Politics*, Vintage, New York, 1996

Best, George, *Blessed: The Autobiography*, Ebury, London, 2002

Bouton, Jim, *Ball Four*, Collier, New York, 1990

Braudy, Leo, *The Frenzy of Renown*, Oxford University Press, Oxford, 1986

Brock, Beverley, *Peter Brock: Living with a Legend*, Macmillan, Sydney, 2004

Chamberlain, Wilt, *A View From Above*, Villard, New York, 1991

Dunphy, Eamon, *Only a Game?*, Penguin, London, 1987

Hazlitt, William, 'Death of John Cavanagh', *The Examiner*, 9 February 1817

Horne, Donald, *The Lucky Country*, Penguin, Melbourne, 2009

Lasch, Christopher, 'The Corruption of Sports', *New York Review of Books*, 28 April 1977

Lessing, Doris, 'My Unwanted Biography', *The Spectator*, 15 April 2000

Liebling, A.J., *The Sweet Science*, Viking, New York, 1958

McEnroe, John (with James Kaplan), *Serious*, Little, Brown, London, 2002

McGregor, Craig, *Profile of Australia*, Hodder & Stoughton, Sydney, 1966

Madox Ford, Ford, *The Good Soldier*, Wordsworth, London, 2010

Marnham, Patrick, *The Private Eye Story*, Andre Deutsch, London, 1982

Nadal, Rafael (with John Carlin), *Rafa*, Sphere, London, 2011

Phillips, A.A., *The Australian Tradition: Essays in Colonial Culture*, F.W. Cheshire, Melbourne, 1958

Rapoport, Anatol, *Fights, Games and Debates*, University of Michigan Press, Ann Arbor, 1960

Stretton, Hugh, *Ideas for Australian Cities*, Georgian House, Melbourne, 1970

Sykes, Tom, 'Why We Adore Liz Hurley's Love Life', thedailybeast.com, 6 April 2011

ACKNOWLEDGEMENTS

Grateful acknowledgement is made for permission to quote from the following published material: Cricket Australia, for the quote from the Big Bash League website; Hardie Grant Books, for *The Future of Cricket* by John Buchanan (first published 2009); Mainstream Publishing, Edinburgh, for *Shane Warne's Century* by Shane Warne (ISBN 9781845964153); Shane Warne's management, for the quote from Warne's website; Pan Macmillan Australia Pty Ltd for *A Golden Age* by Ian Chappell (copyright © Ian Chappell 2006); Penguin Group Australia, for *Standing My Ground*, by Matthew Hayden (2011), and for *Out of My Comfort Zone* by Steve Waugh (2005). Thanks also to Robert Craddock, an esteemed colleague.

Photographs in the insert have been reproduced with the permission of the following:

Patrick Eagar via Getty Images: page 1, top left (Arundel, England); page 2, top left (with McGrath); page 3, both (with Pietersen); page 6, bottom left & right (the jump & drive); page 7, top left & right (here it comes & there it goes).

Michael Rayner/Sport the Library: page 1, top right (Johannesburg).

Jack Atley/Getty Images: page 1, bottom (with Jenner).

Hamish Blair/Getty Images: page 2, top right (with MacGill) & bottom right (with Buchanan).

© AFP: page 2, bottom left (with Steve Waugh); page 5, top (with Mark Waugh).

Ben Radford/Getty Images: page 4, top left (West Indies).

Deshakalyan Chowdhury/© AFP: page 4, top right (India).

© Reuters: page 4, bottom (MCG); page 5, bottom (after diuretic).

Getty Images: page 6, top left (with umpire); page 7, bottom three images (with umpires); page 8, top left (the bad boy).

Adrian Denis/© AFP: page 6, top right (weighing options).

William West/© AFP: page 8, top right (the loved one).

Alex Coppel/© Newspix: page 8, bottom (with Hurley).

While every effort has been made to locate copyright holders, the publisher welcomes hearing from anyone in this regard.